TIBET'S FORGOTTEN HEROES

THE STORY OF TIBET'S ARMED RESISTANCE AGAINST CHINA

BIRGIT VAN DE WIJER

AMBERLEY

*To those heroes who gave their lives for their country;
and to all Tibetans, who should never forget
this part of their history...*

First published 2010
Amberley Publishing plc
Cirencester Road, Chalford,
Stroud, Gloucestershire, GL6 8PE
www.amberley-books.com

Cover: Sherap Sangpo from Jampaling settlement.

British Library Cataloguing in Publication Data.
A catalogue record for this book is available from the British Library.

ISBN 978-1-84868-985-5

Typeset in 10pt on 12pt Sabon.
Typesetting and Origination by Amberley Publishing.
Printed in the UK.

CONTENTS

PREFACE

When reading the history of China's invasion of Tibet, it becomes very clear that nearly the whole world was uninterested in Tibet. Moreover, Jawaharlal Nehru, the then Indian Prime Minister, had a pan-Asiatic dream which made him please the Chinese and boycott all the Dalai Lama's attempts to inform the outside world about what was really happening in Tibet.

It was the era of the Cold War, the Cuba crisis, Korea etc. and the Tibet issue was simply not a priority for the western countries. But even in Lhasa, the *Kashag*, the Tibetan Cabinet, had no intention of giving any support to the eastern regions that were invaded first. This laxness (or was it insipidity?) in combination with the lack of a high performing communication network, an insufficient number of modern weapons and the numerical power of the Chinese resulted in a real genocide.

For many years the Dalai Lama has been emphasizing the importance of preserving the memories of Tibetan people by writing them down. The Department of Oral History of the Library of Tibetan Works and Archives (LTWA) in Dharamsala (India) has been recording since 1976 interviews with elders, Lamas and all kind of people, and possesses an oral archive of 15,000 hours. Some of its recordings have been transcribed, and some are translated into English.

Over the last years, several ancient freedom fighters have been writing down and publishing their stories in Tibetan (see bibliography).

This book about the Tibetan resistance is meant to honour those brave resistance fighters, the *jabmak*, who have tried to face the invader in a long-lasting guerrilla until many of them had no other option than flee to India.

I wanted to keep their experiences alive, so that the Tibetan youngsters of today, and the coming generations, will always remember what their grandfathers or ancestors have done for their country. Next to it, this important part of Tibetan history should also be known by the 'outside' world.

Interviewing these forty-eight 'forgotten heroes', living in three refugee camps in Nepal, has been an unforgettable experience. After so many years, you could still feel the courage and the determination of these warriors; they nearly all expressed their willingness to return and fight again for their country.

It is sad to believe they might never catch a glimpse of their homeland again ...

ACKNOWLEDGEMENTS

Thanks to the Andrugtsang family, relatives of Gompo Tashi Andrugtsang, the former leader of the *Chushi Gangdruk*, for their permission to publish large excerpts from his biography.

Very special thanks to Phuntsok Dolkar for your ever-lasting energy in conducting the interviews, writing down the dozens of translations and sending me lots of precious information by email; to Tsewang Gyaltsen for proposing to give me a hand while you were on summer holiday and giving the best of yourself; to Late Tsultrim and Tseten Kama Sonam for your perseverance in this arduous task during numerous afternoons. Without the precious help of each of you, this book would simply not have existed!

Thanks to the more than a dozen Tibetans in India, Nepal, and in Belgium: Chime Dorjee, Ngawang Nyima, Samten, Chime Lhundup, Karchung Metok, Rinzin, Tashi from Lo-Drik-Tsug office, involved in the interviews, the translation work, the research on place names, etc.

Thanks also to Caroline for your help at an early stage of the interviews, and to Willem for your continuous and professional technical support during all stages of the writing of this book.

Thanks to the Tibet Museum/Department of Information and International Relations in Dharamsala for giving me the permission to reproduce their precious pictures, especially those of the Dalai Lama during his escape; and thanks to the following persons for their authorization to publish pictures from their own private collection: Mr Tenzing Sonam, Lhamo Tsering's son; Geshe Yungdrung Gyaltsen, president of Chushi Gangdruk India; Mr Norbu Dorjee and Mr Kunga from Paljorling camp and Mr Tsering Siten from Tashigang camp in Nepal.

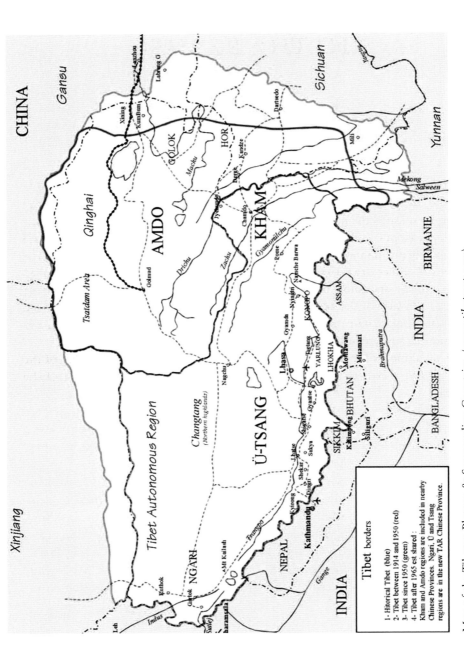

Map of the Tibetan Plateau & Surrounding Countries. (*www.tibetmap.com*)

TO THE READER

Throughout the interviews, hundreds of place names are mentioned. On the advice of the Research Department on Tibet Affairs in Dharamsala, we have mentioned the names as they were used before 1959. Not only have the Chinese given Chinese names to all the places, but, for example, a name which used to be the name of an area became the name of a city, and vice versa. The way the names are written in this book is the way the interviewees used to know them, since most of them never returned to Tibet after 1959, and so are not even aware of the new names. For that reason, we also have opted not to put the Chinese name next to the Tibetan. A few names, however, couldn't be identified, and are indicated with * in the text.

The endnotes for both Part 1 and Part 2 can be found at the back of the book. The words in italics are explained in the glossary at the end of the book.

Tashi Phuntsok (left) and Samphel (middle) spinning wool – Forgotten Heroes.

'From generations of soldiers and government officials on my father's side I inherited a belief that no life was more satisfactory than one of selfless service to your country – or Humanity.'

From: 'This I Believe', a radio broadcast in 1954 by Dag Hammerskjöld.

PART 1

HISTORICAL BACKGROUND

The present is the time of the Five Kinds of Degeneration in all countries. In the worst class is the manner of working among the Red People.

Testament of the XIIIth Dalai Lama (August 1932)

I

GROWING RESISTANCE

In 1949, the People's Liberation Army (PLA) sent troops into western Tibet and *Amdo*; later, in 1950, they invaded *Kham*, the south-eastern region of Tibet. At first, the Chinese soldiers behaved respectfully towards the local people and distributed clothes, blankets, tools, medicines, cigarettes and even money. They did everything to help Tibetans and gave the impression they were not interested in taking over; soon, however, it became clear that a new era in Tibetan history had begun, namely one of repression, atrocities and ... resistance.

More soldiers arrived, and the Chinese began to impose 'democratic' reforms, which was

> the misleading term they used to eradicate the entire social system, customs and religion, and to replace it with sterile communes rigidly controlled by hand-picked Party men. It was intended to sound the death-knell of our religion and the end of the Tibetans as a distinct race and nation.[1]

Moreover, they attempted gun control and disarmament, which made both Amdowas and Khampas furious, since weapons were their pre-eminent status symbol. They refused to co-operate with the Chinese and decided to fight them, despite the repeated urging by the Dalai Lama and others in Lhasa that there should be no resistance to the Chinese.

> I am from Derge, I fought there from 1956, there was a big war in Eastern Tibet. At that time, Tibet was divided in three parts: Kham, Amdo and *U-Tsang*; while U-Tsang was the seat of the Dalai Lama, he had no power of government in Kham and Amdo; his power went only till the river Drichu, one of the four rivers mentioned in the name of *Chushi Gangdruk*. Drichu is important for the Chushi Gangdruk, because that river divided Tibet into two parts; Drichu is the border between inner and outer Tibet. In Meshoe,

a district of Derge, I fought about eight months against the Chinese; they killed 300 Tibetans, but we killed as many of them. While only very few of us had a gun, most of the men had a sword. The three main leaders at that moment were Andrug Phuntsok, Atribhu and Phuntsok Rabten. They were all killed during this war that lasted from 16 January 1956 until the end of August.

At that time, I was twenty-five years old. Only twenty-seven escaped from Meshoe, all the others have been killed, captured or surrendered. All together there were maybe 3,000 people, including women and children. My whole family was also killed, the twenty-seven that were left, were all youngsters that could run. There was no time of thinking of the family at that time.[2]

In 1956, two big monasteries in Kham were bombed. The monks of Chatreng had taken in thousands of villagers to help them to protect their monastery against a Chinese attack. But, with a single airplane, it was bombed and in ruins, while hundreds of monks and laymen were killed. The news spread like wildfire, and the local people gathered in the Lithang monastery to safeguard it against destruction. In the meantime, 25,000 Chinese were heading towards Lithang. The siege lasted nearly two months. Finally, the Chinese issued an ultimatum: either the Khampas should surrender, or the monastery would also be bombed. Half of the Tibetans slipped away at night; afterwards, the monastery was bombed and razed to the ground. About 4,000 men, women and children were killed. The destruction of these monasteries clearly revealed the Chinese intention to control the whole area; it resulted in an exodus of Khampas to Lhasa.

ATROCITIES

The whole of Eastern Tibet revolted against the Chinese, but they replied with more atrocities: women were raped, monks were forced at gunpoint to have intercourse, some were dismembered, vivisected, beheaded, burned or dragged to death by horses or vehicles. Parents were shot by their traumatized children.[3]

People were also forced to attend *thamzings*, 'struggle sessions', an inhuman and sadistic method that added a new dimension to Chinese torture. It was used to denounce anybody of any authority: village headmen, as well as Lamas and landowners. The 'accused' victim was dragged onto a raised platform in a square in town and humiliated by the public, who had to say bad things about him or her. They were severely beaten before and during this session, and often executed afterwards. The Chinese went from house to house, forcing everyone, even children, to attend these meetings. Those who resisted were liable to be the next victims.[4]

There were 10,000 people fleeing from Gawa, they had taken all their belongings and cattle and they were fighting on the way to Jogung, which is a kind of a plateau where we stayed for fifteen days. We heard that the Chinese were coming and we, four to five persons, were waiting on a mountain to see from which side they would come. Then there was this airplane that was so close that we could see the persons inside and we started shooting and the plane crashed.

Then two other Chinese airplanes came and threw bombs; at the same time troops came from all four directions and started killing men, women and children, some 2,000 to 3,000 people were killed. The way they killed was horrible: pregnant women were slashed so that the baby fell out, lots of women and children were killed; if you want to give a good description: it was like hell.[5]

GUERRILLA FORCE

The area of Lithang, and the wider Kardze county, played a crucial role in the establishment of the 'Khampa' guerrilla movement that lasted for two decades. Although in the beginning the guerrillas were not organised at all and had only few weapons, they were highly motivated, excellent riders used to surviving in difficult situations and instinctive fighters who had learned to wield a sword at an early age. The monasteries and the Mimang[6], a clandestine anti-China movement, helped them to improve their systems of communication, supply and armament. By the autumn of 1956, tens of thousands of Tibetans were fighting as guerrillas in Eastern Tibet, and attacked the Chinese army camps, trucks on the PLA supply route, etc. In Lhasa, the Dalai Lama and the Tibetan government were very reluctant to help the Khampas; they feared that the revolt would also spread to central Tibet. Although the Kashag fully realised the gravity of the situation, it was left to the Khampa and Amdo traders living in Lhasa to gather support for their compatriots.

In 1957 the situation got worse and Andrug Gompo Tashi, a businessman from Lithang decided to organise a unified resistance. He devised an ingenious plan to gather the local resistance leaders without alarming the Chinese or Tibetan government and without compromising the Dalai Lama. He proposed to perform *Tenshug*, a religious Long Life ceremony for the Dalai Lama with gifts and prayers offered to him. It was agreed that a golden throne would be offered at this occasion. Gathering donations for this ceremony would provide the perfect cover to organise the resistance without raising Chinese suspicion; in fact, the person responsible for the sponsoring of this event had to travel across the country to collect money from all the Tibetans. For the first time, all Tibetan people were united in a common purpose, which helped to identify the common enemy.

In his autobiography (Appendix 3), Andrug Gompo Tashi relates:

People made contributions generously and whole heartedly. As a result of the contributions a golden throne weighing 3,164 tolas of pure gold studded with many priceless precious stones was created by the sheer hard work and skill of many artisans. A golden "Dorjee" or the symbolic thunderbolt was fixed in front of the throne which alone weighed 133 tolas. The completion of the throne was celebrated with religious offerings. Cash and ceremonial white scarf were presented to the people who worked to create this throne. The throne was offered to His Holiness on 4 July 1957 which was considered an auspicious day. Thousands of people watched the most important ceremony which still continues to linger on in the memories of those who witnessed it. The throne was placed in one of the balconies of the Norbulingka Palace, and when the Dalai Lama sat upon it there was general rejoicing. A 75-tola golden wheel, with eight good luck symbols and many other gifts were offered to His Holiness, who recited prayers and blessed the people. The officials of the Dalai Lama decided to keep the throne in the Potala Palace and the ceremony repeated every year, when the Dalai Lama would sit on the throne and receive the people in audience.[7]

I was the main intermediary between the Tibetan government and the Chushi Gangdruk, a sort of diplomat to report about the situation in Kham and to request aid from the government. It was difficult for them to help us because of the Chinese, but we were secretly given weapons kept in the monasteries, like in Gaden Choekhor monastery. Between 1955 and 1959, I went thirteen times from Kham to Lhasa to report personally to Namseling, secretary of the Minister and to Minister Bonshoe Sawang. Sometimes I travelled by horse, later after three years a road was constructed and I went by Chinese truck from Po through Chamdo to Lhasa.[8]

RESISTANCE MOVEMENT

On 16 June 1958, under the leadership of Gompo Tashi, the inauguration ceremony of the resistance movement, called the Chushi Gangdruk, 'the Four Rivers and the Six Ranges'[9], took place in Drikuthang in Lhoka, a few days travel south-east of Lhasa.

This new organisation had its own flag, with crossed swords on a yellow background; the main aim was to defend Buddhism (yellow colour) from the communist Chinese. The flaming sword being the sword of Manjushree (a bodhisattva, an emanating enlightened being in Buddhism, associated with wisdom, doctrine and awareness), it veers the roots of ignorance, which was the root cause of communism. The other sword, being the symbol of bravery, was the only weapon that the Tibetans could make themselves.[10]

Flag of the Chushi Gangdruk. (*Collection of Geshe Yungdrung Gyaltsen*)

Gompo Tashi and Chushi Gangdruk troops in Lhoka. (*www.chushigangdruk.org*)

Rank among them was all-important. The 'Pombos', commanders, could only be approached with humble respect. Discipline was based on respect and the strict, unwritten code of tribal obedience. All soldiers were under solemn oath never to reveal their actions to anyone, even under torture.[11]

Lhasa was not able to support the continuing influx of Khampa refugees, and many of them started to move to the area of Lhoka. Even central Tibetans started to realize what was happening in their country. Many of them joined hands with the Khampas, and also moved to Lhoka to fight.

In the meantime, in the East, truckloads of children were deported to China for education, so even more women and old people fled from these areas to Lhasa. By the end of 1958, 15,000 families had set up their tents in and around Lhasa.

TRAINING IN THE US

In the meantime, Gompo Tashi contacted Gyalo Thondup, the second eldest brother of the Dalai Lama, who played the role of intermediary with the American Central Intelligence Agency (CIA). The Americans were keen to find ways of supporting the Tibetan movement as part of their global anti-communist campaign. The project was known under the secret codename 'ST-Circus'. The CIA agreed to train Khampas; the first group was sent for training to the South Pacific, but the second one was brought to America, namely to Camp Hale in Virginia, a former Second World War military base in the Rocky Mountains, in the state of Colorado.

> We were kept in different houses for seven or eight days. The attendants of Gyalo Thondup came to brief us in rotation, and tell us to do this and not to do that, we were not allowed to go out, they purchased food for us and we had to cook ourselves and then they would tell us from time to time what to do and when we would leave. One day they told us to be in a particular place at a particular time and not to tell anybody and to be there with nothing else in our hands. Just like that. Suppose we are five in our group, we were told to go to one place and one huge jeep picked us up without any questions, there were already a few people in the jeep and then the next stop a few people were picked up, this huge jeep took all twenty-one of us plus the driver, it was Gyalo Thondup himself, he was driving the huge black jeep and took us to Silguri and then from there we walked for eight hours to the border of Pakistan. We reached there after midnight, maybe at 2 or 3 a.m.; we were picked up by a truck of a CIA agency, I think it were Pakistani people, military top who took us to a small railway station, it was not a

real station, there were only three compartments just for us and we were put in the train with one policeman in each compartment. The train took us to a nearby airport and then another military top came and they put us in a truck and took us to a military airport where American people and an American aircraft were waiting for us. We stayed there the whole night, had American food, like packed food and the next morning we left from there with twenty-one group members and one American to receive us. We flew to the US via Japan where we stayed three or four days in an American base called Okinawa; we had a physical check-up and then we left. One person didn't pass the check-up, he was not fit for parachuting and he was sent back through the same way.[12]

Over several months, they were trained in guerrilla tactics and espionage, in the use of weapons and explosives, in radio operations, survival techniques, map reading and compass work.[13]

The main part of the training was how to operate a radio transmitter and a receiver to send a message, a coded message back and forward, and then also basic military training; it all took six months. The parachuting itself, we practiced it for about five days and then jumped three or four times and that was it. It was no problem, but when we jumped from the airplane in Tibet, it was a big problem; it was high, I think about 5,000 feet high and then there was the wind: the doors of the aircraft, both sides were open and the wind was blowing from both sides, it was scary, but during the practice it was nothing, only 500 feet high and we just jumped one after another.[14]

Since the Tibetans could not write or read English, a special 'telecode' book was created, in which Tibetan words and phrases were encoded into numbered code groups. This became the basis for the Morse Code they would send and receive from Tibet.

One time [during his training in the US] a Mongolian *Geshe* came to teach us Tibetan for a few weeks, he taught us grammar, because we had to know this to be able to send the messages; they were made out of coded numbers that we had to decode into Tibetan because we didn't know English. We had a sort of dictionary with five digits numbers that had a meaning; and so we got all the important words in Tibetan in alphabetical order, all the necessary words. So you got a sentence [in English], then you looked for the Tibetan meaning and you put a five digit number and then you added another number that meant nothing but was necessary to separate the words and so you continued until you had a full sentence. Then the message was received by the CIA and they decoded it and used the same dictionary. I

think the Mongolian Geshe who taught us the Tibetan grammar was also
from CIA side and decoded the messages. This dictionary was made by him
and I think the CIA still have it.[15]

Once their training was completed, they were parachuted back into Tibet in
small groups. Among them was Lhamo Tsering, Gyalo Thondup's right-hand,
who would later head the operations out of India.

While the situation in Lhasa became extremely tense, Gompo Tashi decided
to challenge the Chinese army and joined the resistance leaders in Lhoka. In
July, a first airdrop of CIA arms was made. Unfortunately, these weapons were
not sufficient for the large number of freedom fighters gathered in Lhoka.

[smiling] I will tell you something new that you don't know. There are two
parts in Kham: while Eastern Kham was first occupied, Southern Kham was
still free. When the Chushi Gangdruk was formed only some of the Khampas
stayed in the camp of Drikuthang, most of them went to Eastern Tibet to
fight. There were several military base camps: Damshung, Chakra Palbar,
Markham and Lithang; these were bigger than the Chushi Gangdruk base
camp in Drikuthang. From these places some Khampas have been sent to
the US for training, and later those who have been trained by the US, were
dropped back in these places. Between 1958 and 1960, only two people have
been dropped in Lhoka together with military supplies. Seventeen people
were dropped in Chakra Palbar, the biggest Tibetan military camp. Four or
five military supplies were dropped there by the US. In Damshung (northern
part of Kham), nine people have been dropped; in Markham, ten people were
dropped; in Namtsokha, near Lhasa, eleven people were dropped, but they
didn't meet any Chinese or local guerrillas ('kyye-mag'), so empty-handed
they escaped to India. In Toe Nyari Garthok (western part, near to Ladakh),
six people have been dropped, but they all disappeared; nobody heard about
their fate. In Lithang, six people were dropped. From the people dropped in
Chakra Palbar, four could escape; only two of them are still alive: Donyo
Jagortsang living in Bir (Himachal Pradesh, North India), and Lobsang
Thakpa who is in Bylakuppe (Karnataka, South India); all the others died in
the war. The one who was dropped in Markham, Bumsang, he was captured
by the Chinese, but after his release, he escaped to India; last year he was
seriously ill and came to the Delek hospital in Dharamsala, but I don't know
if he is still alive.[16]

Airdrops! There was a huge wooden pallet, on which they put about ten
boxes and then they dropped it with a parachute. If nothing happened to
the parachute, then the pallet would reach the ground safely, if anything
happened, then the whole pallet would be destroyed, damaged. All the rifles
were packed in cardboard boxes, three in each, the ammunition was also

packed in boxes, then we had bazookas and machine guns, grenades, bombs like C3, C4, TNT, all these different materials for making bombs, fifty and seventy heavy guns, on the pallet everything was tied together with ropes.[17]

For a long time, the young Dalai Lama had not been aware of the resistance movement getting support from the CIA, but when he came to know, he did not give his approval. Nevertheless, when the Chinese asked him to set off the Tibetan army against the resistance he refused, saying the soldiers would surely join the rebels.[18]

Gompo Tashi's forces continued to attack the Chinese in a series of battles, until Chinese aerial attacks stopped their offensive. In February 1959, he reorganised his movement into small guerrilla units that very successfully attacked the Chinese soldiers guarding the main supply route between Xinjiang and Lhasa; this highway looped through south-western Tibet, close to the Mustang border.

UPRISING IN LHASA

In March 1959, Lhasa contained more than 100,000 people, three times its normal size, as many pilgrims came to the capital for the greatest of the religious festivals, the Monlam festival.[19]

At that time, the Dalai Lama completed successfully his final Buddhist examinations, and was invited by the Chinese General Dan Guansan to attend a theatrical performance in the Chinese army camp on the outskirts of the city. The following instructions were issued: the Dalai Lama should come without his customary contingent of twenty-five soldiers, his route was not to be lined with troops, nor were his bodyguards permitted to join him inside the Chinese camp to be armed, which was all very unusual, and the visit should be kept secret from the public. To please the Chinese, the Dalai Lama intended to go without informing the public, since he felt they would disagree. But the news spread like wildfire, and on 10 March, thousands of people thronged the *Norbulingka*, the summer palace of the Dalai Lama, and formed a human shield to prohibit him from leaving his palace, and to protect him with their bodies.

> During the Uprising, I was in Norbulingka, from Derge only there were ninety-two people and there were many people from all parts of Eastern Tibet. We were divided in several groups to guard the palace since the Dalai Lama was still inside. There are four big gates: the southern gate was guarded by people from Derge, Gonjo and Chamdo, the eastern gate by people of Dhargay, Karze, Tongkor and Dawu, the northern by those from Tsawa Rongba, Lithang, Bawa, Pashoe, Nangchen and Riwoche; the western was guarded by people of five different parts of Amdo. Near to this gate there was also the security army of the Dalai Lama.[20]

The Chinese were furious with the Dalai Lama for not accepting their invitation and not being able to calm down the crowd. The situation in Lhasa became literally very explosive: two Chinese mortar shells exploded in the compound of Norbulingka. The Dalai Lama finally consulted the oracle, which advised him to flee. On the evening of 17 March he fled in disguise with his family and some of his closest tutors.

ESCAPE OF THE DALAI LAMA

The Dalai Lama escaped through the southern gate and his security army accompanied him until he reached the Tsangpo [river]. Most of the people didn't know he escaped, except those who were with him. When he crossed the river, the army returned back; at the other side of the river was the Chushi Gangdruk army waiting for him together with the Tibetan government army. The next day, on 19 March, sixty people, twenty from each division from Derge, Gonjo and Chamdo were sent to Rama Dukha to guard the boat to prohibit the Chinese to cross the river. I was also among them. Around midnight on the 19th, the Chinese started to bomb Norbulingka, and on the 20th at 2 a.m., early in the morning at Rama Dukha the sixty people fought with the Chinese. Only one small division of the Chushi Gangdruk guerrilla army came to help us, the leader was Amdo Kelsang. In Lhasa, Chakpori[21] and Norbulingka were bombed and destroyed, all the people ran to Rama Dukha. Near this place was a whole area covered with dead horses and human bodies. I thought that on earth nobody had been left alive.[22]

In his biography, the Dalai Lama describes his escape:

On our way down to the river, we passed a large crowd of people, and my Chamberlain Thupten Woyden Pala stopped to talk to their leaders. A few of them had been warned I was leaving that night, but of course the crowd in general did not know. [...] We crossed in coracles [vessels made of yak skin stretched over a wooden frame]. On the other bank we met my family. [...] About thirty Khampa soldiers were waiting for us, with three of their leaders: Kunga Samten, Tempa Thargye, and a very brave boy of only twenty called Wangchug Tsering. [...] By day we divided into several groups; each night we stopped in a village or a monastery. Sometimes we had no guerrilla leaders with us. They came and went, keeping in touch with all the isolated bands who were living in the mountains, and we knew that we were surrounded by

The Dalai Lama on his flight. (*TibetMuseum/DIIR*)

faithful determined men whom we never saw. Not all of them knew whom they were defending. [...] We stayed for the night in a small monastery at Chenye, but everyone advised us to go on one more stage – to another monastery called Chongay Riudechen – before we made our halt, because that was a bigger place and we would find it easier from there to get in touch with all the guerrilla leaders. [...] Soon after we left Chenye we saw a group of horsemen coming towards us, and as they approached us we recognised among them Tsepon Namseling, one of the officials who had been sent by the cabinet seven months before to persuade the Khampas to give up armed resistance, and who joined the Khampas and never came back to Lhasa. [...] But the devastating news he brought was that Lhasa had already been bombarded. [...] So we went on, and our journey was even sadder than before. [...] But before we left Chongay, I had a most welcome chance to meet some more of the leaders of the Khampas and talk to them frankly. In spite of my beliefs, I very much admired their courage and their determination to carry on the grim battle they had started for our freedom, culture and religion. I thanked them for their strength and bravery, and also, more personally, for the protection they had given me. I asked them not to be annoyed at the government proclamations which had described them as reactionaries and bandits, and told them exactly how the Chinese had dictated these and why we had felt compelled to issue them. By then, I could not in honesty advise them to avoid violence. In order to fight, they had sacrificed their homes and all the comforts and benefits of a

The Dalai Lama, his younger brother Tenzin Choegyal and entourage on their flight. (*TibetMuseum/DIIR*)

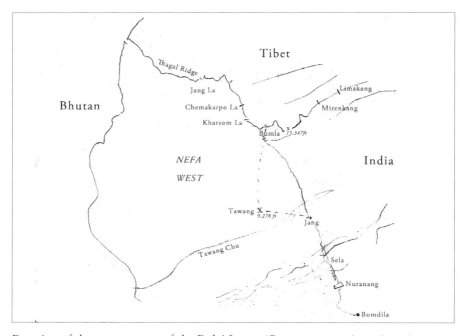

Drawing of the escape route of the Dalai Lama. (*By anonymous interviewee*)

peaceful life. Now they could see no alternative but to go on fighting, and I had none to offer. I only asked them not to use violence except in defending their position in the mountains. And I was able to warn them that our reports from Lhasa showed that the Chinese were planning to attack the part of mountains where they were camped, so that as soon as they felt they could leave me they should go back to their defences. [...] Mangmang is in a corner of Tibet. There is only one track leading to it, and that was well guarded, because we had left some hundreds of Khampas and soldiers at the last place where sidetracks joined our route. Now, unless they bombed us from the air, the Chinese could not take us by surprise or cut us off. [...] The second morning I was still too ill to ride a horse; yet we thought we ought to move, in order to relieve the rearguard of Khampas and soldiers of their responsibility. So my followers helped me onto the broad back of a dzo, the cross between a yak and a cow; and on that primeval Tibetan transport I left my country. There was nothing dramatic about our crossing of the frontier. I saw it in a daze of sickness and weariness and unhappiness deeper than I can express.[23]

Someone present when the Dalai Lama crossed the border relates:

It was in the night from 8 to 9 March that he crossed, in Bumla, it's in NEFA, the North Eastern Frontier Agency which is now Arunachal Pradesh. There was a small inspection bungalow, at that time it was a trader route between Tibet and India. About 300 Lamas crossed the border from different passes, some with the Dalai Lama and some through other passes like Jang La, Kharsom La, Chemakarpo La, Mirenkang and Limakang and they all gathered in Tawang and in Jang. Together with the Dalai Lama entered more than sixty yaks that carried gold, jewellery and some precious stones, some in boxes and some in bags. I don't know what it was exactly. From Bumla till Tawang it was approximately 20 km. They stayed there a little while and then crossed the Tawang Chu, which is a very small but deep river with a wooden bridge. They arrived in Jang, from there they had to climb the mountains again because Tawang is in a valley, it's at 9,278 feet while at the border side it's 15,347 feet. On the 9th, they crossed Sela, another high mountain range, then they rested a little bit in Nuranang and moved on again.

On 10 March, they arrived in Bomdila, it's more than, I cannot say it exactly, 100 km from the border. It was a two days journey sometimes by yak and sometimes by foot, but he was young at that time, he was my age, twenty-four or twenty-five, he was one or two years older than me [the Dalai Lama was born in 1935, he was twenty-four years old]. From there a helicopter was waiting and brought the Dalai Lama together with some important ministers or VIP's like the Home Minister, the Chairman and Speaker, to Tezpur in Assam and from there by plane to Delhi. I stayed with him till Bomdila. The others

The Dalai Lama and his entourage at the Indo-Tibetan border, 1959.
(*TibetMuseum/DIIR*)

came by foot to Tezpur and took the train; some went to Delhi, some to Nilgiri
in Karnataka, some to Dehradun. I think they were 500 in total, but 300 were
together with the Dalai Lama. They were protected by the Indian army, it was
a small army because we only became independent in 1947, and didn't need a
big army in that area since India and China were friends at that time.[24]

The escape of the Dalai Lama triggered a massive military operation by the
Chinese, who brutally quelled the revolt in Lhasa; more than 10,000 people
were killed, and tens of thousands were imprisoned.[25]

No one knows how many people were killed during this onslaught; but a
PLA document captured by Tibetan freedom fighters during the 1960s stated
that between March 1959 and September 1960, 87,000 deaths through
military action were recorded. (This figure does not include all those who
died as a result of suicide, torture and starvation).[26]

IV

SURRENDER

The Khampa guerrillas who had escorted the Dalai Lama returned immediately to continue their struggle within Tibet. By the autumn of 1959, the major part of Tibet was under control of the Chinese, but there were still several centres of resistance in Kham. The CIA continued with their airdrops: between 1957 and 1961, 500,000 pounds of arms, ammunition, radios, medical supplies and other military gear were dropped in more than thirty airdrops.[27]

It was midnight exactly 12 o'clock, we reached safely in Chakra Palbar, we thought that Chinese troops might already be in the area, the CIA didn't know for sure, so they picked out three different places and the three groups to jump there the same night. So we, the three group leaders, sat together and we came to the conclusion they should drop us all in the same place, then we asked them to provide us with a silencer gun, third point was they kept on emphasizing to keep everything secret, especially the CIA involvement, so we asked them to give us a suicide pill because if we would be caught and the Chinese would torture us, we would naturally talk and reveal all the secrets. And first they didn't agree with us on the ground that if we went all to the same place, if there were Chinese then all three groups were caught or killed; if we were dropped in three different places, even if two groups would be caught and killed, one group still might be safe. At the last moment they agreed to drop the three groups in the same place and to give us the suicide pill but they didn't have this silencer, but we didn't believe it, we didn't believe all of it. Then we had to get up at 10 p.m. and get ready and they brought this suicide pill and tied it around our wrist and in case we had to use it, we could take it with our mouth and just bite on it, it was just a small plastic bottle, with liquid inside, half full and not colored, and it was protected with a thin wire, you could easily break it with your teeth; the moment you crushed it, they said you'd be gone. And then we still didn't believe about the silencer and that we were going to be dropped in the same place, they told my group to jump first and then the aircraft would go round and come back and drop the other two groups, we thought it was just an excuse, but it was true. They dropped us and before we reached the ground, the aircraft made a round and dropped the other two groups and that's how we reached there and there were no Chinese, only Tibetans and they heard the aircraft going up and down so they thought we were Chinese troops who were parachuted and so they were running away.[laughing] [...]

From the seventeen people that were parachuted, five of us could make it to the Indian border, the rest got killed, all of them in different places, except three that got killed in the same place. We escaped together to India. [...] It was quite a hard life, our main problem was food, we lived on raw meat, we had to steal animals and kill them; it was the survival of the fittest and even before we reached the Indian border for about seven days we didn't have any food, we only had water and some eatable plants that we boiled. [...] Actually, when we arrived at the border we had nothing but a pistol, a rifle, some ammunitions, that was all we had. Even no blanket, nothing, we didn't take off our shoes for months. Luckily I had my American military boots that I was wearing when I was dropped; all of my colleagues they didn't take care, they had given them to other people. I had kept them. I didn't wear them till we had to leave our horses and had to walk; then I took off my Tibetan shoes, threw them and wore my boots. They lasted till here and I left them with a friend in Misamari, he took them to Mustang and used them for several years. These were very strong, comfortable boots.[28]

The freedom fighters were outnumbered by the Chinese troops and powerless against their sophisticated airpower and communication network. The food and ammunition supplies of the rebels were low, lots of them were injured, and too physically or psychologically exhausted to carry on with their battle. They decided to flee to India, and make new plans from there.

After receiving CIA weapons. (*www.chushigangdruk.org*)

V

ARRIVAL AND
LIFE IN EXILE IN INDIA

At that time, thousands of Tibetans fled from Tibet. Most of them were in bad shape: often nearly dying or wounded, ill from the difference in altitude and not fully understanding they had lost their country. Two transit camps were established: Buxa Duar, a former British prisoner-of-war camp near the Bhutanese border with thirty concrete barracks, and Misamari near Tezpur in Assam, with 300 bamboo barracks where thirty to forty, sometimes up to 100 people were living. Newly-arrived refugees were brought into the camp by truck.

> We walked all the way from Tibet, for one and a half month to the Indian border, even from the border we walked many days and then the Indian troops took us from there to a big camp in Assam that is called Misamari, where all the Tibetan new refugees came together. Thousands of them died due to the new environment, the new food and, I think the water was not very clean in that area because it was bombed in the Second World War.[29]
>
> Misamari was a sordid enclosure with all the appearance of a concentration camp, access to which was forbidden Europeans. Fifty per cent of the Tibetans interned there died in the first year as a result of neglect and of the hot, unhealthy climate, quite unsuitable for Tibetans. It eventually led to the declaration at the Dalai Lama's headquarters that the refugees could hardly be worse off at home under the Chinese.[30]

Lack of clean water, inadequate sanitation and huge changes in food and climate resulted in diseases like dysentery and TB. People were dropping like flies. The Dalai Lama pleaded with Nehru to look for a new place for the refugees where the climate was less damaging, so arrangements were made to bring them to Sikkim (North India) to work on road construction. But it was hard labour. A few refugees preferred, in desperation, to return to Tibet, and face the Chinese again.

Tibetan refugees working at the road, late 1950 and early 1960s. (*TibetMuseum/DIIR*)

A whistle blew at 7.45 each morning and the refugees were divided into groups of ten; men were given axes and crowbars to cut and clear trees, women shovels to dig the roadbed, children baskets to remove dirt and stones. With an hour's break for lunch, they laboured until 5 p.m., receiving little more than a *Rupee* a day, just enough to purchase rice and once a week some meat and vegetables.[31]

Ringchen Tsering remembers:

First we were paid fifty paise [a quarter of a Rupee], later on we got three Rupees a day.[32]

When I was like one month in Assam, we had this meeting and agreed on seven points: to pray for the longevity to the Dalai Lama; to meet the Dalai Lama; to give a special place to the monks and Lamas; to send back the army to fight against the Chinese; to give publicity to the world about what was happening; to provide education for the children and a place to stay for the elders because Assam was too hot. Four of us (Andug Jundak, two others, me) and two Chushi Gangdruk people from Kalimpong, so six people went to see the Dalai Lama in Mussoorie. There all together we did a Long Life prayer for him. We had a discussion about our seven points and handed one copy of our list to him and one copy to the Kashag. Afterwards we went back. The result was that 700 youngsters between fifteen and twenty-five got the chance to study, ordinary people were sent to Gangtok, Sikkim; 1,500 monks stayed in Buxa Duar and the old people were sent to Dalhousie. The Chushi Gangdruk gathered in Kalimpong and they decided to start a new battlefield in Mustang.[33]

Above and below: Ringchen Tsering showing his diary of the year 1957.

VI

A NEW BASE OF
OPERATIONS IN MUSTANG

Life was hard in India, and the refugees started complaining they had not left their country to do this kind of work. Gompo Tashi requested them to have patience. After his arrival in India, he and Gyalo Thondup had immediately proposed to the CIA to revive the resistance inside Tibet, and to establish a base in Mustang (north of Nepal), from where they could send small guerrilla units into Tibet. He had once visited Mustang, and he knew this mountainous area offered several advantages for guerrilla warfare: it was an easy departure point from where they could attack and withdraw, since there were no difficult, high passes along the northern border with Tibet; and moreover, it was close to the Xinjiang-Lhasa highway, which was a vital transportation route for the Chinese. Last but not least, the Mustang kingdom, although officially considered as a part of Nepal, was administered by a Tibetan king, who was naturally favourable to the rebels.

STRATEGY[34]

The initial plan was to send 2,100 ex-resistance fighters who were working in road camps in Sikkim to Mustang. A batch of 300 men would be sent into Tibet to block the highway; another group had to destroy the Chinese military camp of Shigatse (Tibet), and 300 other guerrillas would be stationed near the border to make contact with the groups based in Tibet, and send them extra ammunition if necessary. The transportation of arms and so on would happen by land, and the resistance leaders in India would be informed regularly.

Gompo Tashi discussed this plan with the CIA, who gave the green light to execute it. The plan should be kept top secret; if it leaked and was brought into the newspapers, the CIA support would stop immediately. The road-workers were supposed to be sent in small groups, without knowing where and why they were going. Only after the confirmed arrival of the first 300 men would

Map of Nepal.

another group leave Sikkim. Each person would receive 120 Indian Rupees and a pair of shoes. The arms and all the necessary equipment would be air-dropped into Tibet. It was important to send reliable people and well-trained fighters with a good knowledge of guerrilla tactics, radio signals, etc.

Bawa Yeshi was appointed to be the leader of this new organisation, called Lo-Drik-Tsug, referring to Lo, the Tibetan word for Mustang. He had been a monk in Kham, and had been involved in the resistance since 1958, in Lhoka. He received guerrilla training, together with Gompo Tashi and other leaders in Darjeeling. Later, he met Lhamo Tsering in Kathmandu, where they discussed the new plan.

In the meantime, the first 300 men were sent from Sikkim in small groups of three or four persons, so that if the border security would question them, they could easily tell they were on their way to Kathmandu for pilgrimage, or just wished to avoid India's hot climate. But the rumour of a new resistance army spread among the road-workers. Hundreds of them made their way to Darjeeling until their mysterious migration attracted the attention of the newspapers. The CIA immediately withdrew support.

Soon, more than 2,000 men had gathered in Mustang, where Bawa Yeshi had neither the resources nor the supplies to support them. The situation became even more unbearable as winter approached: the men were forced to boil their leather shoes for 'food', and many of them died of hunger or were frozen to death.

Two people were sent in advance to check the place and afterwards 3,000 soldiers were sent there and each of them received 165 Rupees, a pair of shoes and a map how to reach there. Everything had to stay secret for the Indians so they were sent in batches of fifteen people and after a few days a new group was sent. Unfortunately two groups of 100 army people were caught at the border in Raxaul. Namgyal Dorjee, Gompo Tashi and Chamdo Lonydak were caught in Delhi and imprisoned for three months. They went on sending secretly small groups, also those who had been caught, were sent later on. Some people who were sick, were sent to Dharamsala for treatment; all the others were sent to Mustang. I didn't go, I stayed in Darjeeling to organise this operation. People were sent from Darjeeling and Gangtok. Initially, only 300 persons were to be sent, but all the Tibetans wanted to do something against the Chinese and so 3,000 soldiers had arrived in Mustang. They faced shortage of food and were eating cow's skin and their boots, also it was so cold and they had too much problems, but afterwards they got support from the US.[35]

ARMY LIFE

Twelve instructors that were trained in Camp Hale were sent to Mustang, and arrived in Yarabug on 8 January 1961. At that time the soldiers faced a lot of problems, due to the lack of food and the harsh living conditions. Some older men died in the snow, while others had frostbitten hands and legs, or became snow blind.

In a letter to Lhamo Tsering, the instructors sketch the situation:

Many of them are malnourished and weak since their daily ration consists in only a half pound of rice, wheat or tsampa [roasted barley flour], they only drunk hot water because there are no shops to buy tea, salt or butter. [to make Tibetan tea] Their clothes are in a pitiable condition, they all wear worn-out clothes, so please send them new clothes and a pair of shoes.

The arrival of the twelve instructors boosted the morale of the troops; they were told that they would receive army training, arms, equipment and all necessary support. Four hundred young and physically fit men were chosen and divided into four companies. One radio operator was sent into Tibet to survey the areas where arms and equipment could be airdropped.

In March 1961, the CIA finally resumed aid by dropping arms, supplies and trained Tibetans. In the night of 15 March, two aircraft dropped the expected arms and equipment, as well as eight new instructors. Mainly there were two groups: one actively infiltrating in Tibet, and one giving them assistance by sending reinforcements and making arrangements for food and clothes for all troops.

The Chinese commander, Hen Yung Shen, wrote in his diary:

These guerrillas use the mountainous region, they are disguised as nomads and they generally lie in an ambush not far from the border. They start firing on us, withdraw immediately and don't come back for a second raid. They always send

Soldiers exercising with sticks due to lack of rifles. (*www.chushigangdruk.org*)

spies first, mostly two or three persons to know our positions. We will organise an ambush group under my command and we shall attack the guerrillas. Our group will consist of fourteen soldiers including me, we should be armed with machine guns, a full belt of ammunition, rifles, bullets … and enough food for several days. Everyone should listen to the commander's order and not fire before. After receiving the order, you should fire without hesitation. To know the enemies' position you should catch one or two of them. If the enemy comes with fifty soldiers, they should all be killed; if they are more numerous, you should kill or injure as many as possible and overlook the situation before withdrawing.

The soldiers were well-established in twelve efficiently run camps, under the leadership of independent commanders. They slept in yak-hair nomad tents next to a few modern Chinese and Indian ones. These camps were all stationed away from the villages, near isolated monasteries, or in hidden valleys. Only ill men or those sent down to purchase horses, mules and yaks stayed in the villages.

They owned depots for wood and transport, and a large grain store that contained food that was brought up by mules from Pokhara. In 1964, 6,000 men were under arms in this area.[36]

ARMY RULES

The applied army rules required discipline, respect for the villagers and their belongings, a sense of brotherhood for their fellow soldiers, alertness for eventual spies among them, a complete interdiction on doing business of

selling arms, ammunition or anything else and a total obedience to the orders
of superiors. Violation of one of these rules led to punishments by means
of lashes. A guard who neglected to be alert day and night, and to inform
any anomaly to the base camp, received, for example, 300 lashes from his
commander.[37]

CLOTHES

Tenzin Khedup, one of the surviving Khampas living in the Jampaling refugee
camp (interview 6) explained the guerrillas wore a bivouac cap, often made
from yak leather, touching their shoulders and leaving only their face uncovered.
If it was not too cold, it was rolled up like a bandana. Their shirt, long trousers
and chuba were all linen coloured. In winter time, they wore a woolen shirt
with a light red belt and 'ghora judha', black boots with high heels and laces.

SUCCESS & CHANGING POLITICS

Several raids were conducted along the Lhasa-Xinjiang highway. In October
1961, a Chinese convoy was destroyed in an ambush. Due to the bad condition
of the road, traffic was forced to proceed very slowly. From a nearby hill, the
Tibetans had been waiting until the jeep was below them, and then attacked.
The driver and two others in the front seat – one male, one female – were riddled
by gunfire. When one guerrilla moved forward to take photographs, gunfire
began to pour from the rear of the jeep. The three other guerrillas resumed their
fusillade toward the back of the vehicle. They removed four dead Chinese; they
stripped off their uniforms, shoes, socks and watches. After taking some guns
and a blue satchel containing official documents, they set the jeep on fire. The
satchel, which was sent to the CIA, contained documents showing the extent of
the famine and unrest in China and Tibet, as well as some crucial Chinese army
intelligence and a document revealing that by China's own count some 87,000
Tibetans had been killed during the Uprising of 1959.

Until 1964 numerous raids were carried out until this highway became unusable,
and the Chinese were forced to build a detour further away from the border.

Changing US politics resulted in a fading interest for the support of the
Tibetan freedom fighters. But, in October 1962, China invaded India, and the
Khampas, familiar with fighting in the border area, were asked to join the
Indian army. Because of the Chinese invasion of India, the green light was
given for further US support to the resistance movement in Mustang, but it
was brought under the control of a Combined Operations Centre in New
Delhi and run jointly by an American, Indian and Tibetan representative.

Right: Tenzin Khedup in his former warrior chuba. 'I always kept my chuba because I wanted to show it to my children as something valuable while telling them what I did for the country.'

Below: Chushi Gangdruk warriors in Mustang. (*www.chushigangdruk.org*)

The Tibetans became defenders of their host's borders instead of focusing on fighting for their own independence. In a way it looked as if they were repaying the Indians for their hospitality.[38]

The CIA continued to finance the guerrillas and provide them with arms, equipment and training. The last airdrop was made in May 1965 in Mustang, and although the guerrillas were asked to cease making raids into Tibet and to limit their operations to intelligence gathering, they ignored these orders.

INNER CONFLICTS

In the meantime, problems had risen in Mustang: Bawa Yeshi embezzled the funds received from the CIA while the soldiers were nearly starving from hunger. He claimed that he was saving money in case the American support stopped again. He sent teams across the border to steal yaks and sheep to feed his men, while he pocketed the CIA money for meat. He even began to steal from new refugees crossing the border into Mustang. Gyalo Thondup became aware of this misbehaviour, and sent Lhamo Tsering to calm down the feelings and to establish a financial department. Later Gyato Wangdu, Gompo Tashi's nephew, was sent as deputy commander, but the situation in Mustang deteriorated further, and it was decided to remove Bawa Yeshi. He was called to India and informed about his removal, but he refused a job in Dharamsala and returned back to Mustang, where he organised a split group of about 100 followers.

> When Bawa Yeshi was in India, Lhamo Tsering came to Mustang, he appointed some leaders like Bawa Zeupa and Amdo Kelsang Woser; and they held meetings about Bawa Yeshi's corruption. There were many conflicts and some people committed suicide, like also Bawa Zeupa and Amdo Dolmakyab. Many people were killed, some were told to be Chinese spies, even Lhamo Tsering was considered as a spy. He wrote a letter in the name of the Dalai Lama saying that it was a good thing that all these inner conflicts happened so that the bad guys were eliminated. Chanteng Lobsang Tsultrim brought this letter to Mustang and some people believed it was the Dalai Lama's letter. Like this there were lots of lies, but often they are not told. In my coming book, you will read all these stories.[39]

TRAGIC ENDING

Several political factors, and a possible invasion of Mustang by the Chinese to assure their control of western Tibet, led to the decision to disperse the Mustang forces. Moreover, America and China were trying to get closer and establish

Hotel Mount Annapurna nowadays in Pokhara.

Vehicles for transport business. (*Collection of Norbu Dorjee*)

diplomatic relations. Mao linked two conditions to this: cut off all diplomatic relations with Taiwan and stop all help to Tibet, including in Mustang.

So Gyalo Thondup was informed that the CIA was pulling out of its Tibetan operations, but that they would provide funds to help the guerrillas to resettle in Nepal. Hearing this news, the leaders were so devastated that they decided not to inform the other men. Under Wangdu's leadership, the Mustang force continued for a few more years. In the meantime, Lhamo Tsering worked out a plan for the resettlement and employment: land was bought, carpet factories and handicraft centres were established in Pokhara and Kathmandu, the Annapurna hotel in Pokhara was built, a transport business between Kathmandu and Pokhara and a taxi company in Kathmandu were successfully set up.

Moreover, China started putting huge pressure on the Nepalese king, Birendra (1972-2001), to kick the resistance out of Mustang. At the end of 1973, he publicly demanded that the guerrillas surrender and disband the various camps in exchange for 'rehabilitation' aid and land. Bawa Yeshi agreed to collaborate with the Nepalese in exchange for Nepalese citizenship. The police, alerted by him, caught Lhamo Tsering in the Annapurna hotel and imprisoned him in Pokhara. The guerrillas prepared for the battle, but an emissary of the Dalai Lama arrived with a twenty-minute tape-recorded message in which the Dalai Lama reminded them of the thousands of Tibetan refugees living in Nepal, and asked them to surrender and lay down their weapons. Hearing this message, the freedom fighters were astonished, but had no choice other than to give up. 'How can I surrender to the Nepalese when I have never surrendered to the Chinese?' cried out one of their leaders. So, a few of them preferred taking their own lives by cutting their throats or throwing themselves into the river rather than to face the humiliation of surrender.

Gyato Wangdu escaped with a few soldiers, but was killed by the Nepalese army in an ambush near the Indian border. Lhamo Tsering was imprisoned in Kathmandu for eight years with six other men.

In the book of a Nepalese army officer, this 'Khampa' episode is seen as a terrorist revolution against China supported by India and the US.

> The alien powers had extended cooperation to the Khampa tribes by distributing clothes, food grains, money, arms and ammunitions to them. These provisions were airdropped [...], they had also imparted training to the military personnel. These trainees used to enter the Tibetan land from time to time and sporadically carry out terrorist activities such as raping, massacring people, killing and eating yaks, goats and sheep, plundering, setting shops on fire, etc.[40]

About the tape sent by the Dalai Lama, Dr Prem Singh Basnyat writes that the Dalai Lama incited them to fight against Nepal, but that several Khampas, however, considered it better to surrender to the Nepalese troops (o.c., p.7).

REACTIONS ON THE ROLE OF THE CIA

Tenzing Sonam, son of Lhamo Tsering:

Although it was never the official American policy, the Tibetans were led to believe that they were being trained for the fight to regain Tibet's independence.[41]

Thinley Paljor, who worked as an interpreter at Camp Hale, recalls:

During the training period, we learned that the objective of our training was to gain our independence. In our games-room we had a picture of Eisenhower, signed by him, "to my fellow Tibetan friends, from Eisenhower". So we thought that even the president himself was giving us support.[42]

Sam Halpern, a senior CIA officer at the time, has no illusions about what the aim of 'ST-Circus' was:

I think basically the whole idea was to keep the Chinese occupied somehow [...] keep them annoyed [...] keep them disturbed. Nobody wanted to go to war over Tibet, that's pretty clear. I would think that from the American point of view it wasn't going to cost us very much, either money or manpower. Anyway it wasn't our manpower involved, it was the Tibetan manpower, and we would be willing to help the Tibetans become a running sore and a nuisance to the Chinese.[43]

For some of the Tibetans the American support was a great boost due to their morale: they were impressed the Americans were willing to risk their lives to deliver these weapons and it gave them the feeling they were not fighting alone. There was a lot of gratitude for what the CIA had done for them and their cause. They excused the Americans when stopping their help; no bitterness or any sense of betrayal was shown among the guerrillas, as Buddhists they felt that all situations are transient. Their only regret was that it hadn't started earlier and lasted longer.[44]

THE DALAI LAMA'S VIEW

In his autobiography, *Freedom in Exile*, the Dalai Lama gives his version:

The other sad episode concerned the guerrillas, trained and equipped by the CIA, who continued their struggle to regain Tibetan freedom by violent means. On more than one occasion, I tried to discover detailed information about these operations from Gyalo Thondup and others, but I have never heard the full story. I do know, however, that in 1960 a guerrilla base was established in Mustang, an area which lay in the most remote northern region of Nepal, right on the border with Tibet. A force of several thousand strong drawn from the exile population was assembled there (though only a small proportion actually received training from the Americans). Unfortunately, the logistics of this camp were not well planned. As a result, the would-be insurgents endured many difficulties, though of course nothing compared with the dangers faced by the many extraordinarily brave freedom fighters who carried on the struggle from Tibet itself. When the base finally became operational, the guerrillas harassed the Chinese on a number of occasions and once managed to destroy a convoy. [...] But the fact that there was no consistent, effective follow-up probably only resulted in more suffering for the people of Tibet. Worse, these activities gave the Chinese government the opportunity to blame the efforts of those seeking to regain Tibetan independence on the activities of foreign powers – whereas of course, it was an entirely Tibetan initiative.

In the end, the Americans discontinued their backing for the guerrillas following their recognition of the Chinese government in the 1970s – which indicates that their assistance had been a reflection of their anti-communist policies rather than genuine support for the restoration of Tibetan independence. The guerrillas, however, were determined to fight on. This caused the Chinese government (who must have been considerably troubled by their activities) to demand that Nepal disarm the forces in Mustang, even though there must have been some arrangements between these Tibetans and the Nepalese government. But when they tried to do so, the guerrillas refused, saying that they were determined to carry on even if it meant that they must now fight the Nepalese army as well. Although I had always admired the determination of the guerrillas, I had never been in favour of their activities and now I realised that I must intervene. I knew that the only way I could hope to make an impression on them was by making a personal appeal. Accordingly, I instructed former Kunsung Depon P. T. Takla to take a taped message to their leaders. In it, I said that it would be senseless to fight the Nepalese, not least because there were several thousand Tibetan refugees settled in Nepal who would also suffer if they did. Instead they ought to be grateful to the Nepalese government. They should therefore lay down their arms and themselves settle peacefully. [...] Afterwards, P. T. Takla told me that many of the men felt that they had been betrayed – a few of their leaders actually cut their own throats rather than leave. I was distraught to hear this. Naturally, I had had mixed feelings about appealing to the freedom fighters. It seemed wrong in a way to challenge such courage, such loyalty and such love for Tibet, though I knew in my heart that it was the right thing to do. The great majority of the guerrillas did put down their weapons. But some of them, less than 100, ignored my plea, with the result that they were pursued by the Nepalese army as they crossed from one side of the border to the other. Finally, they were caught in an ambush and met the violent deaths they must have been expecting.[45]

SAMDHONG RINPOCHE'S VIEW

In his book, *Uncompromising Truth for a Compromised World: Tibetan Buddhism and Today's World,* Kalon Tripa Samdhong Rinpoche, the Tibetan Prime Minister in exile, states that war and violence cannot resolve conflicts, referring to long-lasting conflicts between India and Pakistan or Israel and Palestine.

But even Tibetans fought against China. For about twenty years there was a war of resistance. But the result was absolutely nil: loss of so many people's lives, accumulation of so much negative Karma. The only result it did have was a justification for the People's Republic of China to increase repression, to crack down on the people on the basis that there was violent resistance or violent counter-revolutionary activity, an excuse to use force. I do respect their boldness and their courage and their determination and their intention to save the country and its culture [...] actually they were not able to defend anything. They lost. And even supposing that the Tibetan resistance movement had been able to keep the Chinese forces away for quite some time, or even if, due to their resistance, we had not lost our freedom or independence for a long time, that would still only have been a postponement of the inevitable outcome.[46]

THE LO-DRIK-TSUG & CHUSHI GANGDRUK NOWADAYS

Both the Lo-Drik-Tsug and Chushi Gangdruk survived until today, and both became non-violent, social organisations.

Mr Wangyal La, president of the Lo-Drik-Tsug in Nepal:

In 1983, we have established a new organisation here for two reasons: to look after the old people and those who have no family or are in bad physical or mental condition, we give them medical support and good accommodation; the second goal is to give education to the youngsters because my generation is almost at her end and we got no education, so the younger one must not follow this path. This century is an education century, so that's why our organisation supports a good school system and so that lots of students get better education. [interview 1]

In September 2005, the US announced their willingness to resettle 5,000 Tibetan immigrants 'who have been living in Nepal for several years and who were particularly vulnerable'.[47] From various places (people even came from India), Lo-Drik-Tsug people gathered in the Jampaling refugee camp, and some of them even already sold their belongings.

Mr Wangyal La:

The Tibetan administration office told us to collect the names of all the people who were member of Lo-Drik-Tsug because the US was willing to accept Tibetans for immigration. We also collected names from Bawa Yeshi's camp, since Bawa Yeshi apologized. I met his cousin Lobsang Palden in a meeting and he was very happy that we were all United. [interview 1]

Eventually, due to Chinese pressure and Nepalese refusal to cooperate, this immigration program was cancelled.

Lo-Drik-Tsug's president Wangyal La in his Pokhara office.

Old people's home in Dehradun. (*Collection of Geshe Yungdrung Gyaltsen*)

The Chushi Gangdruk organisation has branches in Asia, North America and Europe.[48] On their website, their mission is stipulated as follows:

> to restore independence for Tibetan people through a non-violent movement; to work towards the rights of the Tibetan people to determine their own political, economic, social, religious and cultural future under the sole leadership of His Holiness the Dalai Lama; to preserve the unique Tibetan culture in-exile, which is being systematically destroyed by the communist Chinese government inside Tibet; and to look after the welfare of the veteran Chushi Gangdruk members who are currently living in the Old People's Home in India [situated in the refugee camp Dhondupling in Clement Town near Dehradun in North India].[49]

In Kasur Juchen Thupten's words:

> In 1992, Chushi Gangdruk was registered under the Indian government [Welfare Society of Central Dhokham Chushi Gangdruk]. In 1994, they made a deal with Taiwan about three points; this has been a major mistake and they have been scolded by the Dalai Lama. Afterwards, there were two divisions: the new and the old Chushi Gangdruk. Seven years later, in 2000 they got the blessings from the Dalai Lama and he has forgiven them their mistake. So they became united again. In 2002, a new committee was voted by all Khampas, they have their office in Delhi. [The Delhi office is located in House N° 39, New Tibetan Colony New Aruna Nagar, Majnu-ka-Tilla]
>
> Now a few people in Dharamsala say they are also Chushi Gangdruk, but it's not a real organisation, it's just a name. But, in a democratic country like India, everybody can start an organisation, nobody will stop you, even the three of us (laughing and pointing out to the translator and me) could do that.[50]

In 2008, the Chushi Gangdruk commemorated their fiftieth anniversary; in New York, they were honouring some of the founding members. On that occasion, Kongpo Thubten Dhargey, former Executive of the Chushi Gangdruk, stated that it depended on Tibetans whether they wanted independence or not, and that all people of Tibet should be united. Jamyang Norbu, famous Tibetan writer declared:

> We should remember all the great people who have given up their lives for Tibet; Andrug Gompo Tashi was a genius, we should think like him and adopt his strategies.[51]

Kasur Juchen Thupten.

Donyo Jagortsang.

Looking back after all those years, not all of them share the same view.

> I also fought, I killed more than 200 Chinese; at that time I felt very happy I
> killed so many of them, but nowadays I regret. If you look carefully, the main
> point is that the order to kill was given by a few people, the Communist
> leaders, so the soldiers killed the Tibetans, but if the leaders didn't give
> the order, the army wouldn't kill. Likewise last year some major Uprising
> happened in Tibet [10 March 2008], the Chinese leaders ordered to kill the
> Tibetans.
> But in fact even if I had killed more than 10,000 Chinese, it wouldn't
> have helped. If you kill the Chinese, they also suffer when they are dying.
> So for the next generations we pray that nothing similar will happen again.
> Looking back, there is only to regret about this, because all of this happened,
> nothing is left, only to regret.[52]

Donyo Jagortsang experienced it differently:

> I have a good feeling, although it was a terrible thing that I went through.
> When I think back about the things I went through, I have no regret of what
> I did, because it was a thing that I should have done, although it didn't help
> much, but it was my duty, it was sort of my contribution to the Tibetan
> government and the Tibetan people. It was hardship, all the people I met
> there most of them got killed, caught, went through all kind of terrible
> things; most of my colleagues have been killed, but I have no regret, I am
> glad that I did what I did. [...] I don't feel bad about killing Chinese, in those
> days we believed, it was not a kind of religious believe, it was like a common
> idea that if you killed one Chinese, it was equal like doing some mantra,
> praying. If we think in the way Tibetan Buddhists think, then I am a very
> sinful person not only because I killed but also because I contributed to kill
> Chinese people you know, I was there organising and helping the resistance,
> I was there to get all these weapons, ammunitions, arms to be used to kill. All
> of them were used and how many Chinese have been killed because of me,
> because of us? I'll be the cause of all these sinful things, if you think it that
> way, it's sinful but that's the way life went. Sometimes you have to be very
> religious, when you walk, not to kill any insect and sometimes you have to
> do like that, it depends on the situation.[53]

XI

SETTLEMENTS IN NEPAL

After their surrender, the people of the Mustang force were settled in three different settlements in and around Pokhara: Jampaling, Paljorling and Tashigang.[54]

JAMPALING

The situation in the early years was very harsh, and it was only thanks to the financial support of foreign sponsors that the living conditions improved.

Initially, the only means of livelihood were carpet-weaving and wool spinning, both of which flourished.

> I was sent to Kathmandu to learn this dying and the technique of carpet weaving. I could do this work very fast. I learned the colour combination and designing. In 1977, the first carpet centre opened and I was there and wove carpets. I worked as an allrounder: sometimes as a production manager or I copied the design from the paper. In 1985 and 1986, the carpet business was very successful. [Tsering Siten in interview 46]

But, in the beginning of the nineties, the carpet market collapsed, and other sources of income had to be found. Small projects of agriculture (rice, coffee, banana plantations) financed by western sponsors were started to provide a new income. Some people began their own small shop or restaurant in the settlement. After a decline of several years, the carpet industry saw a small revival, but actually the carpet factory is closed.

At the time of writing there are 479 inhabitants, but the youngsters are leaving the settlement in large numbers in search of a job in the capital, or for studies abroad. There is a day nursery, the Lekshedh Tsal school, with a hostel where nearly 200 students attend classes from Kindergarden up till class VII, a small dispensary, a

Lunch in the old people's home.

gompa, a few small restaurants, and an old people's home, a peaceful haven where the elders without family or unable to take care of themselves are looked after.

PALJORLING

Norbu Dorjee, former camp leader of this camp (interview 23):

> In 1974, 200 to 300 people lived in Paljorling camp. Almost all the guerrillas were bachelor at that time, so when they shifted here in 1974 in one house lived four men. Now there are also wives and kids, so it's getting congested. So we have lots of problems here: we don't have land, we cannot be farmers, we can only survive with small business. All our children are going to school: some are studying in Dharamsala and some in Kathmandu, some are working for the Tibetan government. But, some youngsters leave school after class IX and are only roaming; that is a real big problem.

In this settlement of 442 inhabitants, the Gaden Choekhor monastery counts forty monks; there is a small hospital, an astro-medical institute, a community hall for several activities and the Shree Manjushri Primary School with courses till class V for sixty-nine children, from inside and outside the camp.

Weaving a carpet.

Above: Paljorling
camp in 1974.
(*Collection of Norbu
Dorjee*)

Right: The
settlement nowadays.

Above and below: Houses and gompa in the settlement.

The carpet factory used to employ 100 people, but now the carpet shop employs only a few persons. The large storerooms for the wool are empty now.

A small noodle factory is still producing, but they are not authorised to sell the noodles outside the camp.

TASHIGANG

In this small camp on the outskirts of Pokhara, only seventy-five people are living now and survive on a Lo-Drik-Tsug's pension. There is not any carpet factory or other activity; it's just a peaceful place and a quiet green area.

Tsering Siten (interview 46):

It started in 1975 and it was especially for Lo-Drik-Tsug people. At that time Kelsang from Amdo had lots of contacts and good relations with local officials and this camp was only meant for Amdo people, eighty-five unmarried persons lived here; later Mr Kelsang could not manage the camp well. Some people went back to Tibet, others to India and only fifty-five people remained here, in 1989 it was even reduced to two families. [...] In 1991, the Lo-Drik-Tsug took over the management of Tashigang and started a handicraft centre that was closed in 1997. An office building was also built together with a new residential house where some retired Lo-Drik-Tsug people, called back from Kathmandu, stayed with their families.

Producing noodles.

Lunch in the old people's home: another view.

XII

REWARDS

In December 1992, many of the freedom fighters were received by the Dalai Lama in Dharamsala on the occasion of a 'Tenshug' ceremony. The security office of the Tibetan government-in-exile issued a certificate (see following page) with the following data: a serial number, their name, date of birth, place of birth and father's name, and that the person freely joined the Chushi Gangdruk organisation from 1960 to 1974 and served the country with full dedication. Issued on 3 December 1992.

Above: The participants of the 'Tenshug' ceremony in Dharamsala.

Left: Certificate.

PART 2

INTERVIEWS

Before I depart I must address a few words to the leaders of the Chushi Gangdruk. All of you should unite and take action under the leadership of His Holiness the Dalai Lama. Under his guidance all of you must constantly work with flexible determination for the liberation of Tibet, even at the cost of your lives. The torch of Tibetan Freedom Movement must be passed onto the younger generation so that its flame keeps burning and humanity remains conscious of it.

Excerpt from the will of Andrug Gompo Tashi,
leader of Chushi Gangdruk

INTRODUCTION

Each of the men interviewed has told his own story, his own reality, emphasizing his own sufferings, his own hardships, his own memories of what happened half a century ago.

Each of them related the past in his own way: briefly or longer, in a roundabout way or very detailed, with sadness, with lots of manual gestures, with tears in his eyes, while using his umbrella as a weapon, while ceaselessly counting the beads of a *mala*, proudly, laughing from time to time, combatively, nostalgically ...

Each interview – even the briefest – is a strictly personal account that, together with the stories of his brothers in arms, constitutes a piece of the puzzle of this part of Tibetan history.

Each interview tells *his* truth without the historical accuracy of every detail being sure.

My aim was to collect these interviews without intervening in their structure, to be just a 'service hatch' of this precious information. Only minor changes have been done to improve the chronological flow of a story. A spoken language has been used to stay as close as possible to their words.

Although I do not understand Tibetan, while listening to their stories I felt the vibration of their hearts, still beating for Tibet.

THE MAKING OF

Present at a recording session were the storyteller, one or two interviewers, who were young Tibetan male or female students, myself and Caroline. The interview was fully recorded and afterwards literally transcribed in English.

More than a dozen Tibetans, both in Nepal and Belgium, have been interviewing, listening again and again, transcribing and checking more than thirty-five hours of recording.

With enthusiasm, seriousness and perseverance they have contributed to oral history, 'khagyun' in Tibetan.

During the interviews, children or grandchildren were listening attentively to their father or grandfather ... for some of them it was the first time they heard his story.

Lapsang Dorjee & Tashi.

Rinzin & Karchung Metok.

Chime Lhundup & Samten.

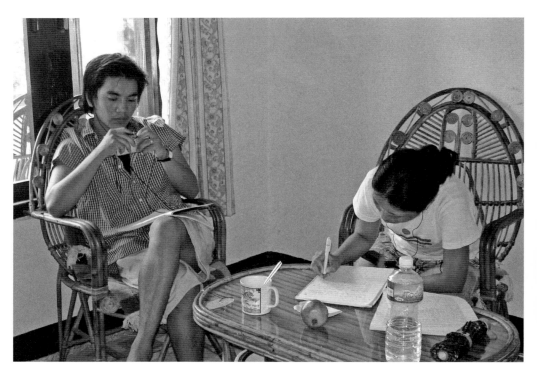

Tsewang Gyaltsen & Phuntsok Dolkar.

Left: Sonam. *Right:* Late Tsultrim.

Choekyi listening to her father Pemba.

III

REACTIONS

Getting involved with the interviews inspired the youngsters:

> I will never forget your kind suggestion in my summer vacation to help you with the interviews, I have the feeling I haven't wasted my time and I gained lots of experiences, knowledge and courage to work for my country by seeing your inspiration. [Phuntsok Dolkar]

> Interviewing the unflinching Tibetan armies with you has been a remarkable event in my life through which I achieved a numerous knowledge and experience for the need of standing up for my country.
> It is heartening to learn the need of collaborative work in your project.
> You really epitomize the patience and perseverance to wholeheartedly bear the difficult conditions of climate and environment to assist the Tibetan people to eliminate their forlorn hope. [Tsewang Gyaltsen]

> I still remember the first time I worked with you was a nice experience. Through your support I became more aware of the old men and their lifetimes struggle. [Karchung Metok]

While visiting the settlements again in February 2009, I took a bound copy of the coming book with me. Everybody was eagerly looking at it.

Phuntsok Dolkar showing the manuscript.

Left: Ngawang Tsultrim with his grandchildren.

Right: Old people's home Jampaling.

IV

INTERVIEWS

	Name	Place of Birth	Region
1.	Wangyal	Lithang	Kham
2.	Lobsang Phakpa	Sog Tsenden	Kham
3.	Kunchok Tentar	Tehor region	Kham
4.	Tashi	Shota Lhosum	Kham
5.	Ahnzin	Jol	Kham
6.	Tenzin Khedup	Shigatse	U-Tsang
7.	Gonchoe	Shopando	Kham
8.	Gompo	Drakyab	Kham
9.	Sonam Dorjee	Rongpo	Kham
10.	Choedak Dawa	Chating	Kham
11.	Tsering Phuntsok	Derge	Kham
12.	Lhundup Tsondu	Namling	U-Tsang
13.	Gyalpo	Jhang Nyemo	U-Tsang
14.	Lundhup Gyaltsen	Jhang	U-Tsang
15.	Bado	Nangchen	Kham
16.	Kunga Chime	Nangchen	Kham
17.	Kelsang Tsering	Dho-Dupte	U-Tsang
18.	Lobsang Monlam	Chungpo	Kham
19.	Dhukhar	Derge Deckyi Ling	Kham
20.	Tsering Dhondup	Toe-Saga-Dzong	U-Tsang
21.	Tashi Dorjee	Toe Choekhor	U-Tsang
22.	Tashi Choempel	Tadun	U-Tsang
23.	Norbu Dorjee	Dartsedo	Kham
24.	Tashi Phuntsok	Namrik	U-Tsang
25.	Pema Lhasung	Nangchen	Kham
26.	Sherap Sangpo	Mangtsa	U-Tsang
27.	Kunga	Derge	Kham

28.	Tashi Topgyal	Lhorong	U-Tsang
29.	Lopa	Gawa	Kham
30.	Tashi Tsering	Gyalthang	Kham
31.	Chime Phuntsok	Drayab	Kham
32.	Dorjee Wangdu	Lhasa	U-Tsang
33.	Phuntsok	Dongpa	U-Tsang
34.	Sangye Gonpo	Kanze	Kham
35.	Samphel	Drakyab Magon	Kham
36.	Jampa Norbu	Tsawa Dzogang	Kham
37.	Jampa Choedak	Jhang Nanning	U-Tsang
38.	Pemba	Nyam	U-Tsang
39.	Pema Dorjee	Nangchen	Kham
40.	Gyurme Dorjee	Toe Ngari	U-Tsang
41.	Takhor	[Not known]	?
42.	Lobsang Dorjee	Gyantse	U-Tsang
43.	Tsering	Narthang	U-Tsang
44.	Yeshi Sherab	Gyalrong Tsenlha	Amdo
45.	Lobsang Tsering	Lungring	U-Tsang
46.	Tsering Siten	Lekshe	U-Tsang
47.	Ngawang Tsultrim	Dakpo	U-Tsang
48.	Dhondup Tsering	Tewa	U-Tsang

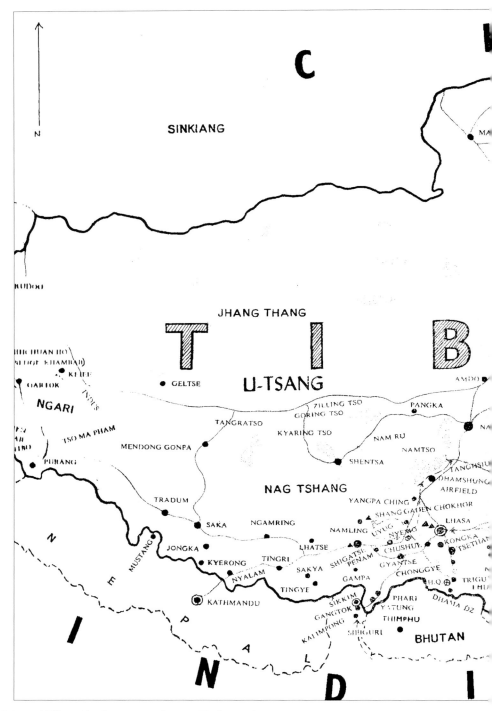

Map of Tibet. (*Andrugtsang, Gompo Tashi,* o.c.)

Wangyal

He has been the president of the Lo-Drik-Tsug organisation in Nepal from
1983 till 1994, and was re-elected in 1996. His life story gives a good overview
of several episodes in the Tibetan freedom struggle.

My name is Lithang Wangyal. I am 75 [78] years old now and I was born
in Lithang in Kham. My father's name was Phuntsok Dhondup and my
mother's name was Sangye Choetsok. I had three brothers and two sisters. I
was monk till I was eighteen and later I went into business. During that time,
merchants from Lithang would bring trade goods with horses and mules
namely, local tea from Kham and material for clothes imported from India,
which were popular in Lhasa.

KILLING IN LITHANG

It was in the beginning of 1949 that the Chinese invaded Lithang; it is
situated near the border between China and Tibet. First they were very
willing to help and support us, but the situation deteriorated soon. Their
behaviour went from bad to worse day by day till in 1958 they invaded
us declaring they came to liberate the people. However, in a merciless and
aggressive way they started killing, torturing and suppressing local people;
they bombed monasteries and vandalised. Continuously there went on big
fights and destructions all over.

At the time the first clash broke out, I was in Lhasa. I later came to know
what happened and returned home. Thousands of monks got killed and also
a large number of Chinese. It was feared that one of the monasteries would
be ruined. So, monks and Lithang people dispersed themselves and struggled
to fight for almost three to four years [months].

During this war, one of my brothers, Ngawang Rabgyal, got killed in a
hand-to-hand fight and another one was badly injured, but he died too after
some days because of lack of good medicine. At that time, I was very young,
but not feeling sad since it highly motivated me to fight the Chinese.

Meanwhile, Chushi Gangdruk's soldiers together with the great Gompo
Tashi secretly started their resistance mission from Lhasa and then to Lithang.
Gompo Tashi made contact with Gyalo Dhondup who himself corresponded
with the CIA in the US. Seven [six] Lithang people were sent to America to
be trained as a warrior. When they came back, Lithang Athar and Lithang
Lhotse had to do some work in Lhasa [make contact with Gompo Tashi and
try to meet the Dalai Lama], while Gyato Wangdu and the four others were
sent to Lithang; one of them had to come overland from India to Lhasa and
by horse to Lithang [one of them, Tsewang had shot himself in his foot and
was in fact unable to jump from the airplane].

People in Lithang were asked to join the Chushi Gangdruk. It was pretty difficult to do it in a covert way because people had to be informed about its purpose; so the Chinese also came to know and they sent more soldiers. In the meantime, the Tibetans were waiting since months for the Americans' military support. By then 40,000 Chinese soldiers, 10,000 in all four directions, were called in to quell further fights in Lithang. After making a plan, Gyato Wangdu and four other people were sent to Lhasa and they reached safely there.

So, with all that had happened in Lithang, I had decided to become a guerilla fighter. I joined the Chushi Gangdruk in Drikuthang where the founder Gompo Tashi launched the first army camp on 5 June 1958 [16 June]. When I was in Lhoka, Gyato Wangdu made an army camp there and Gompo Tashi showed us the do's and don'ts while fighting the Chinese.

SPIES AMONG US

The main reason for the army camp was to help the Dalai Lama escape safely into exile and to avoid him to fall into Chinese hands. When uprising in Lhasa happened on 10 March 1959, I was in Lhoka and on Gompo Tashi's advice 500 men with horses were sent to Gaden Choekhor monastery to collect the weapons. We were able to acquire lots of guns, bullets and gun powder.

On the way back, we met Chinese troops waiting for us near the route to the east of Lhasa. So we went southwards, to Chushul and fought bravely; two Chinese surrendered themselves. Gompo Tashi gave the two a Tibetan name instead of their Chinese one, namely Lobsang Tashi and Tenpa Dhargyal. Some Tibetan fighters were doubtful whether it was a good idea to keep them with us and feed those two strangers; but Gompo Tashi declared that the two sincerely had chosen our side. But in fact they were spying. Lobsang Tashi kept saying to Gompo Tashi to be careful with Tenpa Dhargyal, but the former thought he had become jealous with him; he even gave Tenpa Dhargyal a horse and weapons; but in Chushul, Tenpa Dhargyal fled to Lhasa with his horse and guns. During that short period among the Chushi Gangdruk he had already learned all kind of secrets. Lobsang Tashi repeated he had warned Gompo Tashi and told him they had a big problem now since the Chinese knew their plans.

CONTINUOUS FIGHTING

Afterwards, continuous fight broke out in Dukha Sumdo and Tsang Nyemo. We used to fight during the night, so we hid and waited for the Chinese troops to come and then fought them; lots of Chinese and Tibetans were killed. During that time we suffered so much because we didn't have food and not really a place to hide. During our fight in Mashung, Gompo Tashi was not with us.

Lobsang Tashi told us the Chinese never have compassion; so we should be careful to fight them because when they just use guns, they can only kill a few of us while the others can run away, but when they know where we are, they will throw a bomb on us and kill us all. Afterwards the Chinese indeed threw a bomb on the Tibetan army group, but only a few Tibetans were killed. I really believe that each of us had a personal protector thanks to an enormous cloud of dust that surrounded us.

I heard that Tenpa Dhargyal who was with the Chinese army, had reported to the officials in Lhasa that both Gompo Tashi and Lobsang Tashi had been identified dead during the fights and that Lobsang Tashi possessed a black horse. Gompo Tashi consoled the remaining fighters saying not to feel sad or depressed but to continue to fight. And if it would really become impossible, we knew there were three different ways to flee to India.

Then, we reached Gyasho Bendhar, a place in Kham. The Chinese arrived from two directions, namely from Chamdo and Lhasa. So, we took another route through Nagchuka where we met some locals and villagers who gave us butter, meat and tsampa. We stopped for two or three days to feed our horses. Then we arrived in Chaguthang and traveled further to Shota Lhosum through Chakra Palbar where we made a new army camp. We tried to collect people in Shota Lhosum and around 300 new fighters joined us and received a training. Then we went to Powo Tamo where the Chinese had built an army camp with an office and more than 1,000 houses. At one side of the river there were a lot of Chinese, while at the other there were, I think, only fifteen or sixteen soldiers. We were able to defeat the latter ones easily and kill them all. Then we started attacking the big group, but it was really unbelievably difficult. After feeling something strange was going on, the Chinese troops gathered from four different directions. They had built a tower and made a ditch [tunnel system] from where they were firing at us and they didn't come out for more than ten days. They didn't surrender even though we warned them several times to come out. Instead, more Chinese troops came from Lhasa and Chamdo and we couldn't continue to fight them, so we withdrew and returned back to Shota Lhosum.

We had heard about a secret Tibetan army camp in Tsawa Pashoe and we tried to get some weapons and bullets there; we only got forty bullets and 100 very old Tibetan guns, but it took five minutes to prepare the next shot and you only killed one person at a time. We were 400 warriors whereas only a few of the 300 from Shota Lhosum had brought a gun.

Then we thought to go to Lhoka, but it was impossible because the Chinese army was everywhere but we cheated them by sending a letter in which we announced we would go to Chamdo and Nagchuka, so that food and everything could be prepared for us [by the local people]. Of course most of the Tibetans always did their best to welcome us. So the Chinese went to Chamdo and Nagchu and we could go to Lhoka. Then we went to two different places by splitting in two teams. In Kongpo, we installed an office where we kept all the weapons, one team went to Nagchu, the other blocked the road coming from Chamdo. At that time the leader was Gompo Tashi and he indicated us the official positions. We got food and all kind of support from Kongpo and we destroyed three Chinese trucks and we took all their arms and food. Afterwards more than fifty trucks were coming continuously in our direction on their way to Lhasa. I was with the group who were meant to attack and prevent the Chinese troops coming from Chamdo side. We didn't know exactly where to go and we kept on going in the direction of Lhoka during the night. We reached Gokhachozum* and the next day we reached Lhagyari. At Lhagyari, there was a big Tibetan army camp, where we finally got enough food and accommodation.

In the meantime, we were informed that the Chinese in Lhasa were trying to capture the Dalai Lama in Norbulingka. We made two groups: the group of Gompo Tashi was assigned to receive the Dalai Lama coming from Norbulingka and another group would wait for him at the riverside. Then we kept on fighting firmly and retreated to a safe place. So, after some days, the Dalai Lama had reached India via Montawang. In Chumdogyang, there was a big fight with the Chinese and many of them were killed; they threw a bomb but only a few of our fighters were killed and two were wounded. At that time there were so many groups, each group had 200 soldiers.

ESCAPE TO INDIA

Finally, we had to stop the fighting because we were outnumbered by the Chinese troops and we escaped to India.

I just tell you what I know, that's all.

Around the Tibetan month of March 1959, we reached Montawang where we had to hand over all the weapons to the Indian government. We were granted accommodation, rice, dal [lentil soup], sugar, tea and so on. At that time, more than 10, 000 Tibetans lived in tents that were fit for about ten people. People lived together as a family. Most of us were soldiers and monks, there were only few women.

We voluntarily helped making tents for newcomers. Later we tried with a small group to return to Tibet to fight, but the Indian government didn't let us go. Since we had no weapons and were very poor, we weren't able to do anything. We stayed in Montawang about a month, then we were sent in different groups to Misamari to work on road construction [road construction was in Sikkim].

In Misamari too, there were no houses. So, when the number of Tibetans increased, bamboo barracks were built for thousands of Tibetans by the Indian Government with money of the United Nations (UN). The kitchen and the toilet were just behind the barrack; those barracks were roofed by ourselves with a thick layer of dried grass to insulate from the heat.

In Montawang, the way of living and the environment had been quite similar to Tibet, but in Misamari it was so hot that our thick Tibetan clothes were of no use, so we sold them together with our horses. It was so hot and the sun was burning that whenever we went out during the day, we took an umbrella to protect us from the sun. Some people would faint because of the heat, others became sick due to the dirty water. When you washed a white T-shirt, it became black.

At that time, there was a very big good hospital and common diseases like fever, diarrhoea and headache were cured there. I came to know the disease TB that could kill somebody if neglected. In Tibet, I hadn't heard of it. Health workers tested our blood and urine to track TB infected persons.

Then, the Indian government started to send families with children, monks and Lamas to Buxa Duar. It used to be a prisoner-of-war camp when the British occupied India. When India got independent, the houses were empty, so the families, monks and Lamas could stay there; but it was a very bad place.

People below twenty-five were admitted to schools in Misamari and those between twenty-five and forty were sent to Gangtok in Sikkim for road-work. We were issued a refugee Identity Card which gave us the opportunity to move freely and work in whole India. I too owned an ID card; every year this card had to be renewed. I remember someone told me this card was very precious: it gave access to schools, hospitals and any kind of transportation and also a reduction on several things.

I went to school in Misamari because at that time I was twenty-five. We were taught English and Hindi by an Indian teacher and Tibetan subjects by a Tibetan.

After almost one year I set off for Kalimpong [in the district of Darjeeling in the northern part of West Bengal]. After five or six months, some Tibetans told the Indian government: "we cannot continue this road construction, we only want to fight for our country, that's why you should give our weapons back, we want to go home". These Tibetans came from different regions in Tibet and there were twenty-five representatives from these regions. So, they held day-long discussions about the Tibetan cause and how Tibet could be saved. They requested Gompo Tashi to organise their travel back and he replied them to be patient; that it would be discussed little by little and that now they were refugees here.

At that time, the Dalai Lama was in Mussoorie, near Dehradun.

LIFE IN MUSTANG:
HUNGER, TRAINING AND CORRUPTION

Gompo Tashi cooperated with Gyalo Dhondup who had contact with the CIA in the US. They sent twenty-seven Tibetans to the US for training and six other Tibetans were sent for training in the operation of radio transmitter and receiver.

The idea of a new guerilla camp was developed. In the beginning it was planned that about 500 to 700 men would be recruited and the place would be somewhere in the Tibetan border area of Mustang in Nepal. However over 2,400 men were gathered in Mustang. First, they had planned to establish an army camp in Tibet, but somebody informed the Chinese and their army was already there, so Tibetans set up a camp in Mustang.

From the Tibetan government we were given each 160 Indian Rupees for transportation fare, food and lodging; at that time it represented a lot of money.

We left India via Darjeeling, Silguri and Sanauli; at the border the Indian police took our ID-cards back. In my ID-card were recorded the gun and the two pistols I had given to the Indian government [when I entered India]. We headed through Butwal, Pokhara and finally reached 'Zimbuthang' in Mustang. We called it 'Zimbuthang' because of the omnipresence of a kind of grass, 'zimbu'. This place was so silent since no people lived there; at the horizon we could see wild animals like antelopes and deer.

In the beginning life was so terrible since we had nothing to eat. We quickly lost a lot of weight because of the lack of food. Sometimes we could buy yak and sheep from nomads, sometimes we had to eat yak skin because our meat was finished days before. We first burned the skin to get rid of the wool, then we boiled the skin and ate it after cleaning off the furs. It did help us to survive. Some of the soldiers sold their jewellery: golden and silver rings and 'dzi' [stones with white geometric patterns on black underground] were sold or exchanged for tsampa that was shared among the soldiers of one unit. Due to these hard times, each day thirty to forty people ran away; sometimes in groups of two and sometimes three or four. We made a pair of pants and a sweater out of the blanket we were provided; since we were about to go to fight the Chinese there was just no time to use a blanket. During the night, it was so cold that we used bunches of stems and leaves of juniper and cypress trees as mattress and wraps to keep ourselves warm. We had been looking for a long time for something to keep us warm but juniper and cypress were the most suitable alternatives; and so we remembered a long time this scent.

The people who received training in the US came back, some of them through Pakistan, some through India; and they traveled to Mustang to give us guerrilla training. In Mustang we were divided in fourteen groups; and each group was again divided in two and had his own administration; all groups had the same rules for fighting the Chinese. At that time the situation was very bad but we were helped three times by the CIA: two times they threw guns and materials into Tibet and one time into Mustang; at that time we felt so brave because we finally had weapons.

In 1960, Bawa Yeshi was the leader in Mustang and Gompo Tashi told us we had to listen to him and to twenty-eight training teachers; these were all our leaders. Until 1965 we heard about corruption between the leaders and that money was taken by Bawa Yeshi. Afterwards, the Tibetan government informed the leaders of an emergency meeting in Delhi about all these financial problems. In 1967, the Tibetan government sent Gyato Wangdu to Mustang as the second leader of the army camp and the Tibetan government tried to bring Bawa Yeshi to Dharamsala by giving him a job as assistant of the defence secretary. But Bawa Yeshi tried to cheat the Tibetan government because at that time there were problems with the accounts. Some part of the groups followed Bawa Yeshi, but most of us followed Gen Wangdu. At that time the Dalai Lama sent a message to Gen Wangdu and Lhamo Tsering: "Money is not that important, we have left much more money in our land when we escaped from there. Let's send Bawa Yeshi to Dharamsala". Bawa Yeshi told them he was willing to go to Dharamsala, but he stayed in Pokhara. He tried to convince some people to attack us. In the end, all his plans didn't succeed, so he surrendered to the Nepalese government.

PREPARING OUR FUTURE

In 1962, me and three colleagues were sent to Pokhara and we had a shop from where all the rice, food and clothes were sent to Mustang. After 1964, we rented a restaurant near [the] Annapurna [hotel], it was not so big but the Tibetan government secretly sent money, clothes and army material through this restaurant. It was coming by flight from Biratnagar, near the [south-east] border and from Kathmandu. From there, we had to carry all these things to Mustang by ourselves or we rented *sherpas*. When we carried the money, we speeded up, it only took us four days; but when carrying something else, it took us twelve days. I did this very often.

At the end of 1975 the owner didn't want to rent his building to us anymore; and told us that, if we wanted to stay, we were obliged to purchase it. First he asked 100,000 Rupees, but after a long discussion we agreed on 80,000 Rupees; at that time it was a lot of money. This money was provided by the army camp in Mustang. We had to buy this place because it was so useful for the transportation of goods. Gen Wangdu used to be a businessman and he had a good knowledge of business, so he told us to rebuild the restaurant and also we built some carpet factories and we owned some pigs and chickens and we sold the eggs. Gen Wangdu knew that there were problems in Mustang but he was already thinking of our future life. He thought we had to buy more land, so we built a restaurant in Badoling near the Indian border and we bought some shops in Paljorling in Pokhara. The main goal was that if there would be a problem in Mustang, these factories would make our future possible. Because Paljorling was getting crowded [and we needed more money and so] the building in Badoling was sold later on and more shops were built in Paljorling. I was the manager of the Annapurna hotel until 1998.

TRAGIC ENDING

In 1970, the US and China started negotiations and so the American support stopped and the Chinese put pressure on the Nepalese government to close the Tibetan camps. In 1974, the Nepalese government wanted us to give the weapons back, but Gen Wangdu wanted to fight and we were also ready to fight, but then the Tibetan representative from Dharamsala Phuntsok Tashi Takla arrived with a message from the Dalai Lama: "be more peaceful and give all the weapons to the Nepalese government and we will find some other solution for the future". So that's why we gave all the weapons back, but Gen Wangdu never wanted to surrender to the Nepalese government, so he went back to Tibet to fight the Chinese; afterwards he wanted to go to India. Unfortunately, near the Indian border the Nepalese police and Bawa Yeshi killed him and his five colleagues. The rest of us handed over all the weapons and surrendered ourselves, but the Nepalese government put our leaders Lhamo Tsering, Jigme, Rara, Nagtrug, Tenzin Jyurme, Tashi and Atsha in prison. They decided to put them in prison alive, because they were the organisers of the guerrilla. In Nepal there is a tradition that on the king's birthday they release some prisoners, so they were released after seven years in 1983 [in fact it was in 1981]. That year the Tibetan government established a new Lo-Drik-Tsug office that is still active today.

Conclusion: Bawa Yeshi was leader of Mustang from 1960 till 1967; then the Tibetan government came to know about the corruption; from 1967 till 1974 Gen Wangdu was the chief leader of the guerrilla fighters. He did a wonderful job and still we really admire him. From 1974 we were living like in a Tibetan colony in Pokhara; till 1983 our leader was Lobsang Tsultrim. In 1983 [1981], the seven prisoners were released and together with twenty more people they went to Dharamsala to account for the expenses from 1960 till 1983.

Bawa Yeshi was very disappointed about what he did and he requested the Tibetan administration an audience with the Dalai Lama. So finally he got the opportunity to meet him in Bodh Gaya, where he related him about what he had done in Mustang and apologized for his mistakes. Then the Dalai Lama announced to everybody there that Bawa Yeshi had done a good job first, but made mistakes afterwards, but that this was possible for everybody and that from now on everything was solved between him and the Tibetan government. Bawa Yeshi was very happy at the end of his life and since then the Tibetan administration office took care of his camp in Jorpati [situated outside Kathmandu] in the same way as they did for the other camps; children got the same education as schools depending from the Department of Education.

In 2007, the Tibetan administration centre in Dharamsala advised us to install a coordinating office for all the refugee camps in Pokhara; to focus on education and to develop the camps. The Lo-Drik-Tsug office which has no political task, we are only helping people, would stay the same as before.

I hope that in the coming elections for the Lo-Drik-Tsug and for a Settlement Officer more young people will apply for these jobs, so that before we die we are able to give some advice and show them how to do.[1]

ADVICE TO THE YOUNGER GENERATION

I find it very important to tell our history of Mustang to the younger generation. In 1983, we have established a new organisation here for two reasons: one for the older and one for the younger generation. Our first goal is to look after the old people and those who have no family or have health problems, we give them medical insurance and good accommodation; the second goal is to give education because my generation is almost at her end and we got no education, so the younger one must not follow this path. This century is an education century, so that's the reason that our organisation made a good school system and lots of students are getting better education.

Interview conducted on 20 till 22 June 2007 in the Lo-Drik-Tsug office in Pokhara.

Lobsang Phakpa

I am 64 years old and I was born in Sog Tsenden County in Kham. My father's name was Ngochung and my mother's name was Sonam Palmo. In my family we were eight members; we were nomads and farmers but I was a monk. During summer our cattle was grazing and during wintertime we worked in the field.

Our monastery was assaulted by the Chinese and we were thrown out. Sixty bombs fell from airplanes and destroyed all the monasteries. I fled into the mountains and stayed there; I joined the guerrilla and caused the Chinese a lot of trouble. Once I was caught and sent to a labour camp for five months. It was so big and could accommodate around 200 people. We were ninety-eight monks and we were given lectures about Mao's ideology and we also had to work hard. Afterwards we were allowed to go outside the camp and we were sent to work in the fields. During that time there were three particular categories of persons that were given thamzings: Lamas, high ranking officials and landlords. I have seen ninety-eight of them being captured by the Chinese. They were beaten, torn out their fingers or slapped in the face; some were hung on the wall their hands bound together on their back with ropes. Later we were able to escape with nine people and I could join the Lo-Drik-Tsug.

I was not with the Dalai Lama on his flight. I only heard the news about his safe arrival in India after three or four months; then I also escaped to India via Mustang. I was not with the Misamari group; afterwards I returned to Mustang.

I didn't go for training to the US, but [laughing] I have seen weapons being thrown from an airplane! Those who did go, came back and learned us the guerrilla techniques: we were taught to destroy, to ambush and to demolish bridges. I am still remembering this fourteen-year long training, the fighting against the Chinese near the border and the to and fro crossing into Tibet and back. When I studied Tibetan for two years in Kesangbug, I faced lots of problems.[1] The reason why we learned Tibetan was because we were responsible for the soldiers' salary and the store's accounts.

Bawa Yeshi was a good person and had the qualities of a leader; he was a good military commander, but when he was asked to go to India, he was not happy and made problems with other people.

ADVICE TO THE YOUNGER GENERATION

I have no specific advice to give, but I should say that you have to study hard and preserve our culture and traditions.

Interview conducted on 17 June 2007 in Jampaling.

Kunchok Tentar

I am 74 years old and I was born in a village in the Tehor region in Kham. My father's name was Tsedub and my mother's name was Lodoe. My parents had nine children, four sons and five daughters and I was the eldest and I was sent to the Nadjok gompa to become a monk when I was only eight or nine years old. My family's occupation was farming.

When I was around twenty-one years old, the Chinese came to Kham. First they were very friendly and gave us money. Later they collected information about Tibetans and our way of living, and started to ask taxes, to take all our weapons and to beat the rich people and higher Lamas. Then there was some fight between Tibetans and the Chinese.

So I left the monastery and I did some small business in Chamdo, in Tengchen and Sertsa. I lived there for three years selling animal skins and some herbal medicines which I collected to sell to businessmen coming from Chamdo and some other regions; this was all for the benefit of my stomach.

BE UNITED

Around 1958, Gompo Tashi and some other Amdowas and Khampas came to Sertsa and told us the Chinese were making things worse for Tibetans, so the time had come for us to be united and fight against them. At that time many business people were present there and they discussed with Gompo Tashi and agreed they would join only after one month; since they had collected many things, they were not able to sell them in one day.

I decided to join them immediately, we were eight together. We tried to sell some things immediately, but we left behind most of our belongings with some family and asked them to keep it so that we could pick it up when we came back later. Some other things we just gave them away. So I was with this group; at that time Gen Wangyal (interview 1) was also there and some other people from Amdo and other regions. There were a couple of leaders, but I don't know exactly where they came from or not even what were their names.

Gompo Tashi told us to consider that while at this moment some of the Tibetans were suffering under the Chinese, some others were doing business and enjoying life; and that was not correct. So he told us to go to Lhasa. When we reached Kongpo, the Chinese were already there and we fought lots of battles. Then our leader told us to move to Lhoka.

When we arrived there, so many Tibetan men, women and children were there; they told us the Chinese had thrown a bomb in Norbulingka and that they had killed many Tibetans; and that therefore they escaped from Lhasa. At that time, I didn't know the Dalai Lama already had fled, but after a few days our leader told us the news.

ENERGY TO FIGHT

We fought against the Chinese for a couple of days in Lhoka and it was really difficult and Gompo Tashi advised us to go to Drikuthang, the main army camp. From there we left to Lhagyari where we stayed just one or two days, then we moved and shifted to another group of more than 300 Tibetan soldiers. In the afternoon, the Chinese surrounded all the hills, we then immediately took another way to Tsona, but before we reached there, we heard the Chinese already attacked Tsona, so we had no other choice than to follow the escape route of the Dalai Lama to Magola. We arrived there in the night and we climbed the snow-covered mountain, this was nearly impossible but we had no choice and had to do it. At sunrise, we finally reached the top. Crossing this mountain meant we already reached India. It was really amazing when we crossed Magola, we heard so many noise from flies and bees and it was so hot there; we really felt like arriving in another country.

Before we reached Montawang, the Indian police asked to hand over all the weapons and in exchange they gave us a paper with a stamp – I don't know what this was for. Then we reached Montawang, and we moved on to Misamari where we stayed for two or three months.

Then I went to Kalimpong to do the road-work. Some months later, I received a message from somebody that they collected volunteers to go to Mustang. I felt that since I was with that group in Tibet, I still had the energy to fight for my country. We had to go to Darjeeling to register our name and identity; at that time Lhamo Tsering was the main organizer and we were sent by train to Raxaul at the Nepalese border, and they told us that if the police questioned us, we had to tell them we were on a pilgrimage.

Then we went to Pokhara and in the morning when we woke up, we found ourselves near a Nepalese army camp. They approached us and asked us where we were going and what we were doing there. We told them we came from India and that we wanted to go to Mustang for pilgrimage, then they told us it was impossible and that we either had to go back to India or to Kathmandu. We discussed a long time and finally we ran away in the night and crossed the hill. In the morning we reached the lake near the police station, again we told them the same story but they never listened to us, so we had a little argument and we ran away. They fired on us and one of us died; then finally we were allowed to pass. So at last we reached Mustang, the place where the base camp was, Tangebug where Bawa Yeshi stayed and the main officers too.

SPYING ON THE CHINESE

From 1960 till 1974, I stayed in Mustang, but my group with fifteen people was sent to Nagi, a place very close to Tibet. There our duty was to spy the Chinese and to report to the main office. We were not allowed to kill the Chinese, so that's why I never got the chance to fight them in Mustang. After ten years, I came back to Mustang, so I don't have that much experience about Bawa Yeshi, but when I was in Nagi, I heard about him making problems there. Then, me and my friend, were sent to Pokhara to clear the accounts of our spending in Nagi with our leader Lhamo Tsering in the Annapurna hotel.

At that time I had a little health problem, because I drunk too much strong black tea. When I got very tired, drinking strong black tea woke me up and gave me energy. So I asked Lhamo Tsering if I could go for a medical check-up to Kathmandu. He gave me permission and after a few days, I left for Kathmandu with my friend; while we stayed there, my health was checked and my friend went back to Mustang. I was alone in Kathmandu and I asked our leader what I had to do, he told me to help in the shop. At that time we had a shop with all kind of drinks. I worked there for two years and afterwards we sold this small shop to start a carpet business. In Kathmandu there were a couple of carpet factories, so I stayed there till 1996; then I retired and came back to Pokhara and I got a room here.

ADVICE TO THE YOUNGER GENERATION

I don't have any knowledge, so it's very difficult to give the right advice to young people, but the young Tibetans have to follow the Tibetan government's and the Dalai Lama's advice; I think that's most important.

Interview conducted on 26 July 2007 in Tashigang.

Tashi

I am 73 years old and I was born in Shota Lhosum in Kham. My father's name was Soepa Gelek and my mother's Palzom. We had a joint family with two aunties, sisters from my father with their six sons and one daughter, and me, who was the only child. We were nomads and farmers.

In 1958, I joined the Chushi Gangdruk in Chakra Palbar in Kham. Gompo Tashi was the leader at that time. We fought several times with the Chinese and we were stationed at Powo Tamo which is very near to Kongpo – Nyingtri. From Chakra Palbar to Powo Tamo it was a two days journey by crossing a mountain. I was not there to fight along, but local people joined the Chushi Gangdruk to fight the Chinese; they were stationed in an underground bunker next to a trench, so that we couldn't see them. Three persons volunteered to enter and to fight them, but they never came back and were killed. Maybe there were like 600 to 700 Chinese for only 300 Tibetans. We didn't have any victory and had to return to Chakra Palbar; from there it took twelve days to reach Lhasa.

In the beginning, nobody knew about the escape and the safety of the Dalai Lama and everybody was worrying and very sad about what had happened. But when we reached Kongpo Bhala, our leaders told us about his safe arrival in India and so everybody was very happy. At that time, we had about 1,000 horses and our moral to fight the Chinese was very high. In the meantime, we also heard that Lhasa was captured by them. Near Kongpo Bhala, the Chinese army disturbed us by throwing bombs from the air, so we started moving towards India. On the way the roads were in very bad condition, there was scarcity of food, but the worst was that there was no food for our horses. When we reached in Maggo, they died from eating the leaves of the takma tree.[1]

In Montawang we received food airdropped by the Indian government, each person received one big mug of rice a day. From there we went by foot to Misamari and reached there after four days.

TRAINING IN THE US

In 1960, I was taken to the US for a three-month army training together with twenty-six other people. Although I know the place, I cannot remember the name anymore [Camp Hale in Colorado]. When I reached there, Norbu Dorjee [interview 23] and some others were already there. On the night we arrived, we were provided with all kind of toilet items and towels and we could also take a warm shower. We were taught how to use small and big arms, how to handle mortars and rocket launchers.

I am extremely grateful to the Americans for their help and I wished they would continue their support now. After getting training from the US, I was laughing with the way we were fighting the Chinese before, it was so foolish. We were twenty-six to get a training, now only two are still alive: me and my friend [Norbu Dorjee]. My nickname, codename during training was Scott. I also remember some names of the American instructors like Mr Tony and Mr Mark.

Afterwards, I was sent to Mustang and became an instructor for four companies of 100 persons each. I was never in a real fight with the Chinese, but my 'boys' fought occasionally with them and I was happy that my training bore fruit. I went to patrol in the border areas, I went spying and then on the base of this information, troops were sent to fight. From my point of view, the differences between Bawa Yeshi and the others were caused by the fact that he was a follower of Shugden[2] whose practise the Dalai Lama advised to denounce, and by the Chinese involvement.

After 1970, I came to Pokhara, to Paljorling where I am living till today. I also helped to construct houses here; we used to collect big sized bricks from the nearby river.

ADVICE TO THE YOUNGER GENERATION

I have nothing more to say to the younger generation, but I would love to give them the training I received from the US. Physically I am old, but mentally I am very young and I can still teach.

Interview conducted on 19 June 2007 in Paljorling.

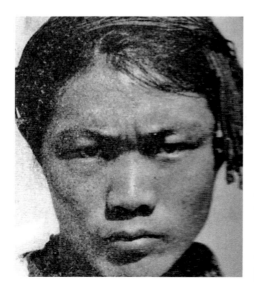

Young Tashi. (*The Lhamo Tsering Photo Collection*)

Ahnzin[1]

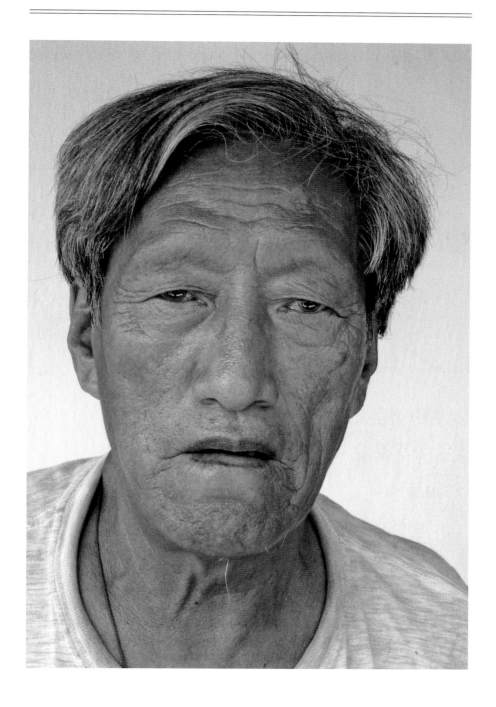

I am 68 years old. My fatherland is Jol, where our Prime Minister of the government-in-exile, Kalon Samdhong Rinpoche was also born and it is in Kham. My family had seven members: two fathers, one mother and three brothers. My two fathers' names were Ahduk and Ahtherbu whereas my mother's name was Palchen.[2]

When I was thirteen, I used to look after the cattle as a nomad; but at fifteen, my father, eldest brother and me joined the army. Looking back, my first memory is that I fought the Chinese since I was fifteen to get Tibet free and to give it back to the Tibetans; and it gave me lots of energy but also lots of suffering. Till now Tibet is neither independent nor given back to the Tibetans, but now I am old and I always tell my children to continue the fighting.

I was eighteen when I left Tibet and went to India. An army group remaining in Toe told my group to come back to Tibet to help them. When we arrived there, the group had already collapsed and the area was occupied by the Chinese. I was fighting China [the Chinese] in Tibet till the age of twenty-one or twenty-two and finally escaped to India. I stayed in Gangtok for one year and shifted to Mustang. So I joined the Chushi Gangdruk organisation at the age of twenty to fight the Chinese.

When I was twenty-one, I fought the Chinese with an axe; because we had no weapons, we couldn't challenge them. If somebody was injured, there was a Tibetan doctor who gave a medicine. It was the same as now.

I think in 1959 I was already in Mustang, but when the Chinese completely occupied Lhasa, I was in India. When the Dalai Lama went from Lhoka to India, we were just behind him.

BADLY INJURED

Actually the Chushi Gangdruk was organised in Tibet by Andrug Gompo Tashi, but then they had to go to India and from there back to Nepal and so they established it in Mustang. But the Nepalese government didn't allow and destroyed the organisation. Then we came here. I fought under this organisation for two years in Tibet, during that time unfortunately I was hit by a sharp Chinese bullet; it pierced my knee mortally and I was grievously injured. I was hospitalized and Tibetan doctors took care of me for one year. Simultaneously, two of my friends were seriously wounded by bullets: one of them, who is still living in Dharamsala, lost one leg, while the other one, who is living in Gangtok, was badly injured. I cannot tell you more about it because it makes me cry …

ORDINARY SOLDIER

I didn't follow any training in the US. I don't know exactly where the weapons came from, but in the night weapons were dropped from the planes at some place in Tibet. It took us two days to walk from Mustang to Tibet to get the weapons and return back. I completely ignore where they came from because I was an ordinary soldier. Our officials ordered us to go and get the weapons and come back.

In Tibet, Bawa Yeshi was not the chief leader but just a leader and in Mustang he became head of the Chushi Gangdruk organisation. Afterwards there were some problems with the group and then Bawa Yeshi and his group just split; I really don't know what the exact problem was, because I was an ordinary soldier at that time.

I stayed sixteen years in Mustang as an ordinary Tibetan soldier. In the beginning the facilities including the food were very poor. For example we happened to boil the skin of a yak and ate it due to the insufficiency of food for all. Afterwards it was getting better, I don't know where the food came from. [I asked him if he knew that rice was brought from India] I know nothing about rice coming from India, because the storerooms were down in the village and we were living on the top of the hill. I have no pictures from Mustang myself but some leaders have taken numbers of pictures at that time. I don't know where they are now.

ADVICE TO THE YOUNGER GENERATION

I always tell my own children that my family was a noble and rich family in Tibet, but that the Chinese stole everything and killed them all. Always remember the atrocities of the Chinese in Tibet, the destruction of the monasteries and the culture and the Tibetan government. If somebody asks you who your father is, you can be very proud, because I made history, never forget what I did. So you have to continue. My mind still wants to do so, but I am old and unable to do any more.

Interview conducted on 10 June 2007 in Jampaling.

Tenzin Khedup

Right now, I reached the age of 70. I was born in Shigatse in U-Tsang. My father's name was Lhakdon [short form for Lhakpa Dhondup] whereas my mother's name was Sodon [short form for Sonam Dolma]. There were seven members in my family: me, four sisters and my parents. Our occupation was agriculture.

I joined the Chushi Gangdruk in 1958. The reason why I wanted to join was because Tibet's condition became worse and the Red Chinese captured our land. I am a Tibetan and I had to take responsibility for my own land.

Of course we knew what kind of atrocities the Chinese did. First, they told the Tibetan people they wanted to develop the land of Tibet and they gave financial support. One or two years later, there were more problems and more suffering and of course this was the main policy why they came to Tibet. To act against this, the Chushi Gangdruk organisation was started. In this organisation were included the people of Cholkasum [= three provinces of Tibet: Kham, Amdo and U-Tsang].

I have always remembered the things done by the Red Chinese in 1957 and in 1959 our country was completely occupied by the Chinese when the Dalai Lama fled from Tibet. Till now, I am feeling so bad, it really looks like a dream or an imagination that we don't have a country. I was not with the Dalai Lama when he escaped from Tibet. There were three groups on the way, each group had more than 200 army men, I was part of the group near Lhoka. There were two other groups of 200 people, for example one in Jampaling and one in Raxaul and one in Paljorling who were protecting the Dalai Lama on his way to the border.

BAD WAY

When we entered India from Montawang we chose a very bad way via Magola; we got lots of trouble there because we didn't find anything to eat, no food or shelter. This way is surrounded by snow mountains. Actually there are three different ways to go to India: through Sikkim and Darjeeling, or through Montawang or Pemakoe and Zayul. That time some people survived but it was too difficult on the way.

I have not been for training in the US. I heard that before the invasion of Tibet some people went there for training. After the invasion, when we reached in Misamari, some of the soldiers who were older than twenty and between twenty-five and thirty-five, could go to the US but they only chose a few people from each group. They chose the most intelligent and of sound body. That time I reached the age of twenty-six, but I didn't get the chance. It didn't depend on our own wish. For example I was selected from U-Tsang, and from Chamdo the most talented and clever people were selected to join in Mustang.

I left my family in Tibet when I fled to India. Till now, I often remember this difficult situation. My conclusion is that since the Chinese came to Tibet, I really feel sad, especially in 1959 when they occupied Lhasa. I feel angry and sad because they are not reliable; they first announced they would help us to develop our country but at the end it was not like that.

We reached Mustang in 1960. There I have no more special experience to tell to you. The main things I had told before. I always want to fight to get my country back.

When I reached in Lo-Monthang we got the chance to go to Jhang two times. That time some soldiers fought the Chinese, but I didn't get the chance.

If I am talking about Bawa Yeshi, I have a long story but I am just telling you the necessary things. The main thing I want to say is, he was the leader of the Lo-Drik-Tsug. Afterwards, between the leaders there was a problem, then he started his own organisation and did corruption of the army salary.

Phuntsok Dolkar interviewing Tenzin Khedup.

ADVICE TO THE YOUNGER GENERATION

I am always thinking that, if my country Tibet gains freedom before I die, I will be very happy. Anyhow I always told my children and my grandchildren, if my generation cannot go back to Tibet, you have to continue to get our country back.

I have no special suggestion to give, because I have mentioned it all before. We had the worst condition when we reached in exile in India and Nepal, but foreign people and the Tibetan exile government are helping Tibetans in our cause for justice, so I have the feeling that still we have some hope that we'll get our country back. Sometimes I feel so proud we have such a wonderful leader as the Dalai Lama. For all these reasons I think that before I die, I will see my own country back. And also I hope the international support for Tibetans will increase and become stronger. For this I would like to pay lots of thanks from the bottom of my heart.

In school when I was a foster parent for three years, I always advised them to do their studies very hard and also the Dalai Lama always keeps saying the younger children are the future. So you have to keep this in your mind. When I meet students on the way doing bad things, I advice them also. If they listen or not, I always advice them that we are becoming old and that they are the future generation of Tibet and have to fight for our country.

Interview conducted on 13 June 2007 in Jampaling.

Gonchoe

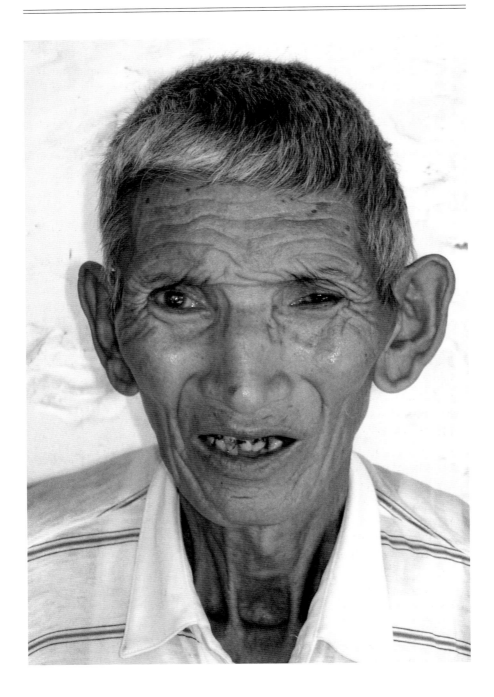

At the time of the interview, he already looked very fragile; he passed away in 2009.

I am 74 years old and I was born in Shopando which is in Kham. My father's name was Bhukya and my mother's was Tsering Dolma. I had three brothers. Our occupation was farmer.

I joined the Chushi Gangdruk in 1959. When I was young, I thought that if I stayed in my place, the Chinese would do atrocities. So I believed it was better to join and to do as much fighting as I could to protect my country. Nobody forced me to do this.

The first time the Chinese people came into my country, they were helping people and bought whatever we needed and started communist propaganda. But then, the situation with the local people became worse: they killed high Lamas and were against religion and they also caught people who didn't want to follow the communist ideals. They even had no compassion on killing women and children.

Later, I joined Chushi Gangdruk, and then I travelled around in other parts of Tibet and could see that the situation was the same everywhere. So we started to fight the Chinese, it was almost impossible to challenge them because of their large number of soldiers.

BOMBING FROM THE SKY

We ran away from Lhoka to Tsona, then we arrived in Magola at the border between Tibet and India. There were more than 2,000 or 3,000 soldiers and the Chinese followed us by airplane and threw bombs, but we were very lucky because suddenly the weather changed and became very foggy so that the Chinese couldn't see us from the sky; otherwise they would have killed us easily. I was with Andrug Gompo Tashi all the time, because I was his security guard. There was also another group, they had to fight the Chinese.

From Magola we reached India, first we arrived in a place named Montawang, then in Bomdila, and afterwards in Misamari. There it was very hard to live; almost twenty to thirty people died every day due to the weather and bad accommodation. We stayed there for two months and we begged the Indian government to send us to some cooler place; so they sent us to Gangtok and to Sahara (India).

One day Andrug Gompo Tashi and Gyalo Dhondup, the Dalai Lama's brother, came to ask us our opinion. We told them that we didn't want to work on the road construction or do work for India, but that we wanted to go back to Tibet and fight against the Chinese so that we could live in our own country. Then Gyalo Dhondup told us: "Now relax, we will work on it". One day they called us and announced us they made a plan to go to Mustang. Later, we reached Yarabug where our Tibetan army camp was established. But this was all very secret; we had told India and Nepal that we wanted to go to Mustang on pilgrimage. There were many groups with people from Amdo, Kham and U-Tsang.

RATIONED TSAMPA

One of my strongest memories is, in the beginning when I was in Mustang, we got lots of problems. First, we had a problem [to accommodate] to the [new] environment, then we had not enough food, so we ate grass or animal's skin. We had a little bit of tsampa, one cup had to be shared with ten people. Even if we had a small piece of meat, we had to divide it in ten. Also we had stomach problems and lots of soldiers got diarrhoea. Fortunately later we got support from the US through the Tibetan government and so we got better accommodation and we also received weapons and all necessary soldiers' equipment and salary. Our situation became better and we had the courage to fight the Chinese. We were always doing guerrilla and we often went into Tibet and killed Chinese soldiers; we hid a bomb under the road, covered it and when a truck drove over it, it exploded. I did it three times and our group made also crash an airplane.

I stayed in Mustang till 1974. Then, due to the Chinese pressure on the Nepalese government, they asked us to hand over the weapons; but we really didn't want to give them. Some of our soldiers said if we give the weapons, then better we die. So between us and the Nepalese government the situation became worse. Then suddenly a representative from the Dalai Lama came to Mustang and gave his message: "Don't worry and give these weapons to the Nepalese government and be in peace". Then we gave them all our weapons. Later, the Nepalese police took us to Nuwakot. Since the prison was small and we were numerous, we stayed nearby but we couldn't move freely, so it was like a prison.

First, our army leader was Bawa Yeshi, later he didn't do good for the soldiers. Then Gyato Wangdu became our chief leader. When we were in Nuwakot, the Nepalese government asked us to join Bawa Yeshi's group, but we told them: "If your government forces us to join, then it's better to die. We want to follow the Tibetan government". So, we never followed Bawa Yeshi's group or listened to the Nepalese government.

From Nuwakot, we were sent to Kotre Khola. There our condition was poor. We had to spin and wash the wool. That time, we got support from the Tibetan government, each day we got three Rupees. This money was collected and spent for the community. Due to the Dalai Lama and the

Tibetan government, our situation became much better. Then we were sent to Jampaling settlement, the Tibetan government made houses to live in and now our situation is wonderful.

ADVICE TO THE YOUNGER GENERATION

The young generation has to know the way of living in Tibet and how to eat tsampa, it also has to preserve our culture and tradition. It's not necessary to copy the western modern attitude and culture, and also not the Nepali one. Do follow the Tibetan government rules, don't use drugs like western and Nepali people.

Interview conducted on 23 June 2007 in Jampaling.

Gompo

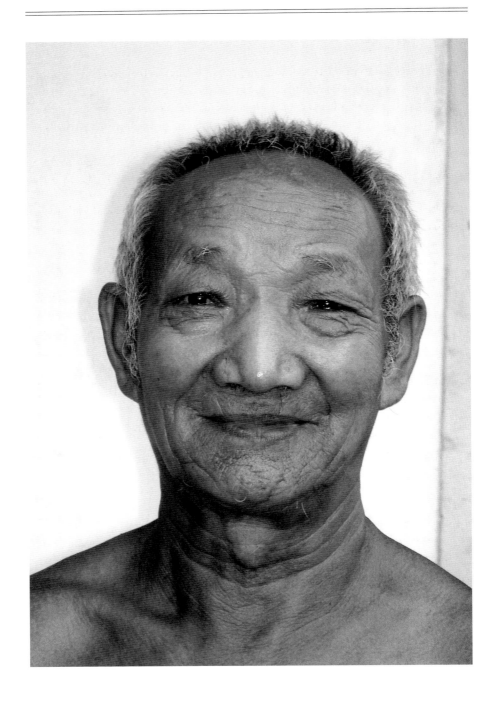

I am 76 years old. I was born in Drakyab in Kham. My father's name was Ata, whereas my mother's name was Samten. In my family were five brothers including me and one sister, but they all passed away. I stayed in the Drepung monastery for seven years. My parents cultivated crops and were rearing cattle as nomads do.

In 1959, I heard about the Chinese oppression in some parts of Kham and Amdo, but I haven't seen any atrocity in Lhasa. At that time, the Chinese gave financial assistance to the poor people in Lhasa, thus they believed the Chinese were supportive and altruistic.

But when the Chinese invited the Dalai Lama from Norbulingka to the Chinese camp, the people knew better than that, so monks and lay people came to surround Norbulingka for seven days. When the Dalai Lama left around 9 or 10 p.m., the Chinese bombed Norbulingka and fought for two days. Three of my friends died and people were also killed by falling trees. Countless people lost their lives in Lhasa. Even four or five months later, when I was in India, I still didn't enjoy my food, because I still had like a bomb taste in my mouth.

I had no knowledge of warfare, since I was a monk. We incited the Chinese to fight, we shouted "Come on, we want to fight", "*faro sagyu*" [which means literally: eat your father's dead body; it is a kind of invective], but we couldn't see them because they had a lot of war experience. The Chinese were shooting at us all the time, they were nearly hitting us, bullets were flying about our ears or landed in front of us but we were never hurt thanks to our *tung-wa*. [talisman]

Then, we wanted to leave, but it was difficult to cross the muddy road. We stayed for two days in Gunri, on the top of the hill in Drepung, then we came down to Chushul. From there, we went to Gongkar, where we voluntary joined the Chushi Gangdruk. I was accompanied by a few people and we had 300 bows and arrows and swords taken from Norbulingka, because at first no one was admitted without weapons.

Gongkar is at two days distance from Lhasa and they have built an airport there. Me and some other persons were sent by the leaders to the other side of the Tsangpo river to be watchmen during one week. And then, the Chinese came to Chushul, and we were fighting them for two days in Pelker Chode [= holy place in Gyantse] and we killed many of them while we only lost two men.

FORCED TO ESCAPE

When I look back at my life in Tibet, the main memory that emanates swiftly in my mind is the unchangeable willingness to fight the cruel Chinese and to get freedom. In the current situation, I have no knowledge about the modern political issue nor am I literate. Thus I constantly dreamt to combat them. When we came to the lake Yamdruk Tso, I boldly told my company about my desire to stay behind a big rock on a hill and fight the Chinese with my old bow and arrows until they were all finished so that I could end my last breath in plunging into the lake. Nonetheless my company rejected my strategy and by taking all my things, they forced me to escape to India together with them. I was very disappointed.

Then we reached Tsona, near the border from where it took one day to reach India. We fiercely fought there for three days. Unfortunately we lost a lot of security guards of the Dalai Lama to whom we had got familiar during our stay at Norbulingka and I also lost a few of my friend monks. I was sad about the death of the security guards because they had family, while monks when they die, they don't leave a family behind.

We reached Pangchen near the Indian-Tibet border where we had to stay around fifteen days. Unavailability of proper food made us eat leaves of trees, while we had in fact money to buy something to appease our hunger. Then we crossed the bridge and went to Montawang, where we stayed one or two months. That time we were so numerous and we got Indian support, in fact I don't know who helped us, but there were airplanes coming with food. Then I went to Misamari where I lived for six months, but it was incredibly hot there.

At that time, a school opportunity was provided for those under the age of thirty; once you became thirty, you had to make your own life. Despite of being twenty-nine, I decided not to join the school because my main goal was to fight the Chinese for a free Tibet, and I had no willingness to live a happy life in asylum.

Afterwards, we went to Gangtok and worked at the road for one year, and there food and everything was provided, but in my mind I was never thinking of building up my life in India. My heart always yearned to flee back to Tibet and to liberate it from the Chinese. I never got the feeling that India was my home.

DIFFICULTIES ON THE WAY

Andrug Gompo Tashi told us: "If you guys, you really want to join, we will not force anybody, you can just join voluntarily". We had problems to leave India, we tried to cheat the border police and paid them. When they watched us, we did as if we were making tea and it looked as if we had no plans to go anywhere, but then at night we escaped and crossed the border. We made our way to Mustang.

In Pokhara we were prohibited to pass for three or four months by the Nepalese police. Then we went back to India and we were kept in Gorakhpur by the Indian police. Again we went back to Nepal and we took a plane from Kathmandu to Pokhara and the Nepalese police kept us there for exactly six months. The Tibetans insulted the Nepalese police and in Naudanda we strongly struggled, nearly fought with them because of their prohibition and we cut the thread that was supposed to confine us. In the nick of time, we reached our final destination Mustang.

Insufficient food made our condition unbearable, we nearly died from hunger but never I thought about stealing or attacking somebody to take food. Our only thought was to go back to Tibet. Sometimes we went to Changtang, we beat and killed Chinese. When we were sometimes successful in taking yaks and so on from the Chinese, we never used them for our own purpose; we always gave it to the leaders of our group. I stayed in Mustang for thirteen years.

BAWA YESHI

At first, Bawa Yeshi was good. His obsession in working with his fellow soldiers and his good cooperation made him the ideal leader but afterwards he became a very bad person and we got very less from the financial support the US and India had given. He kept the monthly salary of the soldiers for his own purpose and blemished the reputation he had built. We got so many support; for example, in India, in Dehradun the Tibetan army got salary and other benefits, we were supposed to receive the same in Mustang; but we didn't receive anything. Bawa Yeshi was a very dishonest person. He took some very important statues from Tibet and some other important things. Gen Wangdu was opposing Bawa Yeshi, we really wanted to kill him but Lhamo Tsering told us not to think about killing people but to negotiate. He said Bawa Yeshi would give all these precious things to the Tibetan government and the Dalai Lama. But he surrendered to the Nepalese, then all this money was his; maybe he took it with him when he died ...

You see now in Kathmandu there are several foundations and factories, all this was done by Gen Wangdu, he was a good leader and a good person. Bawa Yeshi didn't do anything like that, he kept the money for himself, but nevertheless he died.

ADVICE TO THE YOUNGER GENERATION

The Tibetans only have to follow the Tibetan government's 'Middle Way' and keep the Tibetan religion and culture high.[1] I am seventy-six, I have a nephew in Lhasa and he always told me to come back, but I ran away from the Chinese, so I just don't want to surrender again. The Dalai Lama and we got so many support and if I have karma, and Tibet will become free, maybe one day I could go back before I die and then Tibetans will be united again.

Interview conducted on 11 June 2007 in Jampaling.

Sonam Dorjee

I am 68 years old and I was born in a village called Rongpo in Kham. My father's name was Kunchok and my mother's name was Kelsang. I don't remember exactly how many members there were in my family, I think we were seven: my mother and father, my grandfather, two uncles who were monks and, well, all I know is that I was the eldest son. We were '*drokpas*' and had 600 or 700 yaks and 'dris' and around 1,000 sheep and goats.

When the Chinese came in 1959, I was still in Tibet. In 1958, the organisation Chushi Gangdruk was formed and they made a golden throne for the Dalai Lama and the Chinese came to Lhasa and the business people went to Drikuthang and made an army station there. The people came mostly from *Dotoe* and *Dhome* and only a few were from U-Tsang. When we went to Lhoka, we could only travel in small groups. We realized that we could never beat the Chinese since they were much too strong for us and even though we had no weapons, still we felt as if we had to do something, that we had to fight them.

MY STRONGEST MEMORY

My strongest memory is, when I was in Lhoka; I was only nineteen and it was a very hard time but we did a very great job and it was really my best experience in life. *Gyalwa Rinpoche* came through Lhoka on his flight to India, the Chushi Gangdruk already occupied this area and so we helped him to make his way through Lhoka and further to India. Most of the Tibetans who fled to India also passed through Lhoka. We were there with our horses; there were many people and most of us were from Dotoe and Dhome and only a few from U-Tsang. We occupied the border and we were living in different groups. There were also a lot of monks from Kham who had been living in the monasteries of *Ganden* and *Sera* and they had been able to reach there easily. Afterwards a lot of Chinese came from the north to Lhoka, they had lots of weapons and the Tibetans had not enough weapons and only of bad quality and so many Tibetans were killed.

The Dalai Lama was in Montawang escorted by some of us and he sent a message to us through one man called Chatran Wangyal: "Now don't fight, try to help the people as much as you can and then come to India".

In 1959 I fled from Tibet through Assam and then I went to Sikkim. I was only nineteen, we were all young Tibetans and we were kept in Misamari to go to school and in 1960, the Lomagar [army establishment in Mustang] was founded and most of the members were businessmen. That year, we were sent to Mustang.

The CIA was already involved since the time of Lhoka. At that time we got little support of arms by airdropping, but it was not enough; in Mustang we got full support and lots of weapons. I didn't get any training in the US.

From 1960 till 1974 there was not a continuous fighting; sometimes we got information, sometimes we were damaging roads and bridges. This was in Jhang, the north of Tibet where there are lots of nomads. It was not easy to cross the border, but we went through the mountains and during night-time we fought and returned to Mustang. It was not a continuous battle, but only from time to time. It lasted till 1974.

I have no pictures and I think no one does, but some people have a good memory about what happened. Most of the [old] people now here in Jampaling were part of the group coming from Lhoka who 'protected' the Dalai Lama.

Our whole life has been a hard life; life is hard when you have no country.

ADVICE TO THE YOUNGER GENERATION

I am not really experienced or have much knowledge, but all the Tibetans have to follow the leadership of the Dalai Lama and keep convinced faith in him. You have to get back the country and be united among Tibetans.

Interview conducted on 2 April 2007 in Jampaling.

Choedak Dawa

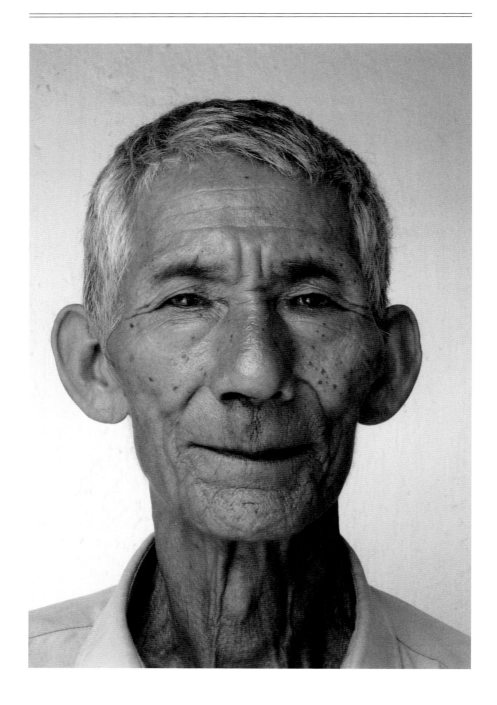

I am 72 years old and I was born in Chating in the region of Kham. My father's name was Sonam Phuntsok and my mother's was Tenzin Dolma. I have three brothers and one sister. My family were farmers and I did small business.

I joined Chushi Gangdruk organisation in Kalimpong in 1958. This organisation was established by Andrug Gompo Tashi. At that time, there were ten people from Chating, ten from Lithang, ten from Bawa and ten from Markham; so all together there were forty people in this new organisation. In Kalimpong, twenty soldiers were given driving training because we would have to fight the Chinese, and we would have to hijack their cars and drive them; while the other twenty soldiers were given nursing course, so that when we were fighting and somebody was injured, we could help them. That time I followed the driving course and I was twenty-three. From Kalimpong we went to Drikuthang without any weapons. From there the soldiers were split up in several groups and we stayed there for fifteen days. Me and a group, we were sent to Lhasa because from Lhasa there is the main road the Chinese were using and we could attack the Chinese trucks. Then we went to Norbulingka.

FLEEING FROM NORBULINGKA

Around Norbulingka there were more than 1,500 people and soldiers. More than 500 soldiers decided to go along with the Dalai Lama and more than 1,000 soldiers stayed in Norbulingka to protect it. At 10 p.m. the Dalai Lama left Norbulingka.

The next early morning at 6 a.m. the Chinese bombed Norbulingka. I was there, more than 600 soldiers were killed and only 400 were left. We escaped from Lhasa and after three days we crossed the river. Actually there is a bridge but the Chinese army was there so we couldn't pass and so we crossed the river by yak. We had only four yaks and at that time there were more than 1,000 people from Lhasa along with us. First one person held the tail of a yak and then another person behind him held the leg of the first person and so we all crossed. Actually the Dalai Lama had no plan to escape from Norbulingka, but all the soldiers and people encouraged him to leave because we knew the Chinese were going to blast a bomb in Norbulingka.

On the way there were so many women and children and we protected them. But at the other side of the river, the Chinese were there and we were fighting them but we had only a few bullets and we couldn't really fight but we were able to reach safely to Chushul. And there we stayed only one night and we wanted to send the people to Changtang, there was a hill between Chushul and Changtang and we crossed it and from there we could pass to India. Four hundred soldiers stayed in Chushul and we sent away the people.

But we couldn't stay in the village because the Chinese were there, so we had to stay at the other side of the river but we had no food or drinks. Five of our soldiers were killed by the Chinese when they tried to get water and food in one home.

After five days, we got a message from the Dalai Lama in Dargula and he told us to try to leave from there. So we escaped from Chushul, the Chinese followed us and threw a bomb but nobody was killed.

When we reached Dargula, Andrug Gompo Tashi divided the army into two parts. He sent us back to Lhasa to fight the Chinese. On the way lots of people were killed by them, only 375 soldiers were left. When we reached Lhasa we couldn't fight them because they threw bombs from the airplane and fought with guns. That time the Americans gave us support of weapons. Usually they first chose where they would throw the weapons, Chakra Palbar was chosen but the Chinese were in Chakra Palbar, so they couldn't throw them there. Most of the soldiers were living in Driku[thang] and they made an appointment to get the weapons there, but it was not possible.

I stayed in Lhasa for two years. The first year we didn't fight the Chinese, the second year we did. That time the Tibetan government promised to give

Crowd around Norbulingka. (*TibetMuseum/DIIR*)

us support of weapons but the Chinese occupied almost all Tibet, so they couldn't. We stayed in Lhoka for three months and fought the Chinese. We couldn't face them because we had no weapons. From Lhoka we went to Misamari in India, after that to Darjeeling where we worked more than one year in the road construction and then to Mustang.

MY STAY IN MUSTANG

We stayed there for fourteen years and when I was there, I had such a great confidence in myself because we had such a good weapons and support from the US. We were like ten groups, sometimes fifteen groups to fight the Chinese. We killed the Chinese and put a bomb under a jeep and we killed as much Chinese as we could. This is only a short expression of what I experienced, it's my strongest memory.

The Lo-Drik-Tsug organisation was first established by Bawa Yeshi, he was the leader of the army camp. I know the Tibetan government transferred Bawa Yeshi to Dharamsala and Gen Wangdu came to Mustang as the new leader. That time Bawa Yeshi took eighteen lakh [1 lakh = 100,000 Rupees] to India. He stole the salary of the soldiers and even their food. He made friendship with the Nepalese government and told them about the Lo-Drik-Tsug organisation and the Nepalese army came to us and wanted to destroy everything. But Gen Wangdu had planned to fight the Nepalese, because he thought they were the same as the Chinese, so we could also fight them. But, then we got the message from the Dalai Lama not to fight but to give back the weapons and surrender. We listened to him and gave everything back and the Nepalese army even took the army's food and clothes, they were robbers. Then, they destroyed the army camp, and sent us to another place.

We really became poor. We had put some money at the Nepalese bank in Mustang, almost six lakh, but we didn't get it back. Bawa Yeshi contacted the Nepalese army and they killed Gen Wangdu, that happened at that time. When we reached in Jampaling settlement we had no money, but I think we got this camp here and that it was paid by our money on the bank.

ADVICE TO THE YOUNGER GENERATION

I always advice the young people to study hard because a life like ours would be very difficult. That's my main advice.

Interview conducted on 16 June 2007 in Jampaling.

Tsering Phuntsok

Since he was not feeling well, the interview was very brief; he passed away in November 2007.

I am 85 years old and I was born in Derge, which is a place ten days from Kanze and four days from Njarong, in Kham. I don't know the name of my father because he passed away before I was born. My mother's name was Lobsang Choedon. I had a father, a mother and a brother and most part of my life, I spent in the monastery. I heard from people coming from Tibet, that all the members of my family died. My family was rich, we worked as farmers and nomads. We had enough fields to cultivate crops like wheat, carrot, etc.

'TO DO OR DIE'

I joined the Chushi Gangdruk after I escaped to India. I hadn't joined in Tibet since I was a monk in the monastery. I heard about the complete destruction of my monastery named Tashilunpo [in Shigatse, previous seat of the Panchen Lama] later, when I was already in asylum.

I escaped after the Dalai Lama, I think around July-August. I haven't seen the barbaric acts of the Chinese during my presence in the monastery. We kept the gate of the monastery closed in order to get rid of them. I heard the news of the destruction later when I was in India and that only one relic of the Panchen Lama was left.

My main memory is that during the Chinese occupation people escaped and faced lots of difficulties and hardships on the way. My experience as a soldier was not so big, only as a guerrilla fighter. In the army we were submitted to follow every word of the General and the device "to do or die".

Obviously, Bawa Yeshi was a leader of our organisation and first he looked very capable but afterwards he wasn't, he took all the salary of the soldiers and all the support and ran away.

ADVICE TO THE YOUNGER GENERATION

I cannot give you much advice, just follow the Tibetan leaders and the Dalai Lama. Whatever they say, you should follow.

Interview conducted on 11 June 2007 in Jampaling.

Lhundup Tsondu

Right now I have reached the age of 65. I was born in Namling which is in the area of Shigatse in U-Tsang. My father's name was Tenzin Wangyal, he was secretary in Gaden Choekhor monastery which is situated in Toe, the upper area of U-Tsang. My mother's name was Sherap. In my family I was the only son, I have no brothers or sisters. We were doing agriculture.

I was a monk in Gaden Choekhor monastery. When I was in the monastery, the Red Chinese did a number of atrocities to us. They came to the monastery and they told we were not allowed to raise the national flag. That time monks were always opposing their orders. We threw stones and pulled down their flag. Like this we have done lots to the Chinese. If we had to fight one Chinese, that would have been possible, but if we killed ten of them, the next day there were 100 of them and if we killed these 100, then there would be 1,000 of them. And 1,000 would change in one million ... We had less population compared to the Red Chinese: there are six millions of Tibetans to six billions [in fact 1.3 billion] of Chinese, but still we were fighting them. I never felt like we were lost.

When I left the monastery, I lived in Nagtshang; there were six different villages. For three years I joined the group of Nagtshang to fight against the Chinese troops. The cantonment was divided into three branches. The Chinese were getting more numerous, so we couldn't win and we fled to Toe. That time we were more than 100 monks. When we fled from Toe to Lo Monthang [in Mustang] only thirty-one people were left, all the others died. Among them all were monks except one layman.

I escaped from Tibet in 1959. I have not been for training in the US; only the elder ones went there and I was too young at that time. But when the Americans helped us with weapons thrown from the airplane, I was together with the elder ones.

Neither was I with the Dalai Lama; the Chushi Gangdruk members helped to escort him from Tibet to India, but we came directly from the upper region of Tibet to Mustang.

SUFFERING FOR THE COUNTRY

In Tibet, the army troops organisation was called Chushi Gangdruk, but when we reached in exile in Mustang, we established a new organisation named Lo-Drik-Tsug which was situated in Yarabug. When we were there, we got lots of trouble and still we were fighting the Chinese almost every day. It was a difficult time, for example we had no food to eat or anything else. We even had to boil leather to eat. Later we ate tsampa which was sufficient for two days. Instead of Tibetan tea, we drank black tea and later we drank tea with 'tsilu' [= greasy meat, normally not meant to be eaten by men]; we considered this greasy tea as tasty. Afterwards, we received some salary from the US and then we had the opportunity to drink a better tea. Sometimes we had porridge for dinner, when we looked into it, we could even see our face. We faced such a poor situation at that time. But, even now I miss the days of the past.

During my stay in Mustang, I was the leader of five army groups and there were different leaders. I was with two soldiers who carried the machine guns and I was the shooter. I stayed in the school named Kesangbug for four years, it was a school in the cantonment, especially for the army and we studied only Tibetan. I also was the secretary in the army group. Sometimes we suffered a lot and sometimes we were happy too. Anyway, we stayed there for fourteen years. I only tell you the important things now, because if I tell you the whole story, it would last too long.

Most of the soldiers were saved due to the precious *Tso Sung* [Tibetan charm box]. Unfortunately, the Red Chinese killed some soldiers even if they wore it, because they had put animal's or women's blood on the bullets; by putting dirt on the bullet, it didn't work properly, since it is sign of peace and blood is synonym of violence, of dirt. 'Tso Sung' can also not be worn by women. Even when bullets were shot on our body, while wearing it, head or other parts wouldn't be hurt.

First, Bawa Yeshi was the leader of our organisation, then later he became our enemy. He did corruption of the salaries of the soldiers given by the US. Each soldier even didn't get his monthly salary, so a conflict took place.

I left Tibet at the age of sixteen and I stayed in Mustang for fourteen years. What I did, I did it always for my country and not for myself, I wanted to

Tsewang Gyaltsen interviewing Lhundup Tsondu.

Lhundup Tsondu wearing his
protection box *(gawu).*[1]

sacrifice my life for my country. Still now I am courageous and bold to fight
the Red Chinese. From the beginning till now I have done great deeds for the
country. I am always feeling sad that I have not my own land, I am a refugee.
Without being discouraged, it blows my mind to get freedom of my country
soon from the Red Chinese.

ADVICE TO THE YOUNGER GENERATION

As per the suggestion of the Dalai Lama the young children are the future
seeds or the future generation to take over the country. So I also think the
same. My main advice is to do your study hard and think about your country.
The elders are becoming old, so raise your courage and inspire yourself.

For it, do your study hard and in between you need a good character.
Preserve your culture, the traditions of your country Tibet. I always tell my
children to be ready and to take their country Tibet by their good education.
Education is the peace builder of the country.

Interview conducted on 13 June 2007 in Jampaling.

Gyalpo

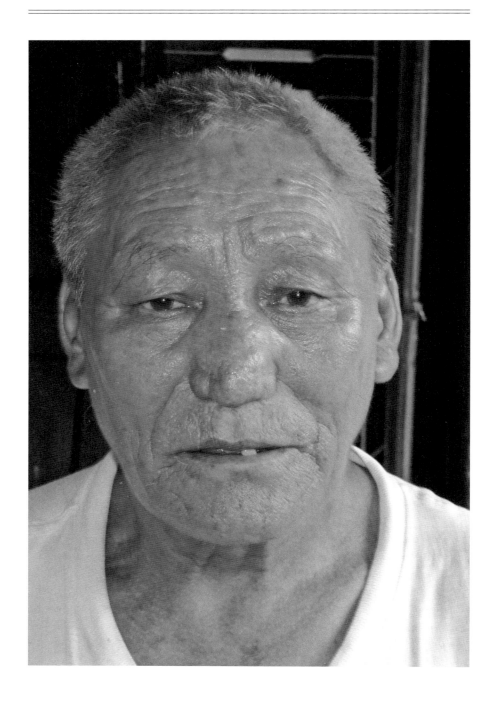

He is a friend of Tsondu and born in the same place.

My name is Jampa Choejor, but they call me Gyalpo. I am 71 years old and I was born in Jhang Nyemo which is in U-Tsang region. My father's name was Dorjee and my mother's name was Kunchok. We were only three members: my father, mother and me. I stayed twenty-two years as a novice monk in the monastery named Gaden Choekhor, while my family lived their life as a farmer.

I joined the Chushi Gangdruk organisation in 1958. The Tibetan government gave lots of weapons to the Gaden Choekhor monks and we kept them in the monastery store room. According to a secretly sent letter by Gompo Tashi to the Chushi Gangdruk organisation, 500 soldiers came to take weapons from our monastery. If the secret leaked out, there was a chance that the Chinese would destroy our monastery. Then, Chushi Gangdruk soldiers along with their leader Gompo Tashi pretended to surround our monastery and declared they were going to put it on fire if we weren't giving the weapons. But in fact, the monks and the Chushi Gangdruk we were on one side. Gompo Tashi told the monks that if they went along with us with the weapons, there was the danger of the Chinese. So we joined them later. For the sake of our country Tibet, five Gaden Choekhor monks decided to join.

When the Chinese came to our monastery, all the monks threw stones and so the Chinese couldn't stay long there. They didn't do any atrocities, but my friend Tsondu (previous interview) stayed longer and he knows all about this.

Me and five monks joined the Chushi Gangdruk in Lhoka because we couldn't stay there because of the Chinese. I thought that if we couldn't fight, at least we could help to make tea and food.

FIGHTING EIGHTEEN DAYS AND NIGHTS

We left the monastery on the 15th of the month of February, fled to Lhoka, from there to Nyemo and then to Chushur. Near the bridge of Chushur we stayed on one side of the river and the Chinese force settled at the opposite side. We fought against them for three days; then we fled to Gungkar, from there to Toelung and there we met Sonam Dakpa, who was a secret guard of the Dalai Lama, and monks of Dargye Gonpo. All together there were thirty-seven monks. Then we all moved to Lhodrak Dowa. To reach there we surrounded the land of Drigu. We had lots of good weapons such as machine guns etc., because of the security guard and some high people who were along with us. Then we discussed that to fight the Chinese was very hard, so instead we decided to put our goods on the horses and fled to India; the Dalai Lama already had escaped to India. But then, all our soldiers decided to stay in the same place till our death and we fought against the Chinese for eighteen days and nights.

Later, we fled to Bhutan, where we were stopped by the Bhutanese government for one month. When they got the information from the Indian government to let the Tibetan refugees free, they let us go. Then, we started our journey to India. On the way we faced a problem of lack of food and so we ate horse meat by killing a horse. When we reached Baksa [near the Bhutanese border], we decided not to stay there, and continued our journey to Sikkim. There we reached in 1959 and stayed there for one year.

We heard that if we reached Silguri, we would receive new clothes and we were not allowed to wear precious 'Tse Song'; so we sold them at a cheap rate. But when we reached Silguri, there wasn't anyone to give us new clothes and precious things, so all our precious things were lost. This information was just a trick for the soldiers to join the army of the Lo-Drik-Tsug. From Silguri, we travelled to Mustang and we reached there at the end of 1960. Again due to overpopulation we didn't get proper food or drink. Then we ate boiled leather and 'thukpa' made of tsampa.

On 15 March 1961, America threw some weapons. From that time, our salary increased for a while and our food facilities improved. We went into Tibet for eleven or twelve times. We went from Narto [near Manang in Mustang] to Gangla. From there it takes more than three hours in the snow to reach the Khung Shanob* pass and then to Wache Trangku* pass. We received the information that the Chinese would arrive in this area around 8 or 9 a.m. They fired on us and there was a fierce fighting from 8 a.m. till 9 p.m. There were almost eighty or ninety Chinese killed and we caught 200 to 300 yaks at the same time and handed them over to the Lo-Drik-Tsug. Several times we went into Tibet as guerrillas. I was not there when they obtained the documents from the Chinese. With these secret documents the Chinese planned to control Tibet and the whole world. They were given to the Tibetan government and were shown to the world; it made the group very popular.

OPPOSING THE NEPALESE

From 1960 till 1974, we have been fighting against the Chinese from Nepal. Then the Chinese explained to the Nepalese government that there were some splittists living in the guerrilla and that they had to remove them, otherwise their relations would be disturbed and also their trade agreements.

So, the Nepalese government was in a difficult situation and decided to bring the Lo-Drik-Tsug organisation to an end and take our weapons. They came to us and asked to surrender and our leader Gen Wangdu declared we were fighting for our country and that since the Nepalese government was a part of the Red Chinese, there was no difference between them and we would fight them too.

The name of our group was Kongra Gyashok [gyashok = group of 100 soldiers]. Other names were Tenzin Gyashok and Didak Lekung, and we were all settled in Lupra area. There we were waiting to fight the Nepalese and they were also waiting, nobody started to fight for six days. After six days, the official Kusung Dapon Takla Phuntsok Tashi from Dharamsala came and along with him a representative from the Dalai Lama from Kathmandu and they brought a tape-recorded message from him. When we listened to it, we were gathered in a group and the voice of the Dalai Lama was speaking: "You have received these weapons from the US and now you have to give them back and avoid bloodshed and you all must surrender these weapons to the Nepalese government. Later, if we get in trouble again, we will receive much better weapons." This information was like putting ice into boiling water and nobody opposed this advice and I went back to my Kongra group and then we surrendered all the weapons and not even a single bullet was left with us.

AFTER SURRENDERING

The Nepalese authorities informed us to go to Kesangbug, because there would be Tibetan and Nepalese officials that would communicate our future resettlement program and say in which place we had to settle. They told us: "You don't have to take your belongings, because you can come back in the evening". In Kesangbug, we were kept two or three days in a group and we were not allowed to go back and we were sent to rug [= Tibetan word for a valley]. Then we were sent to Nuwakot, it was a very bad place in Nepal, it is a prison and we got very bad food.

This was the third time I lost all my belongings: the first time in Tibet, afterwards in Sikkim and now there in Mustang. We stayed there for seven or eight months. They couldn't keep us longer there because it was difficult to feed us and also the Nepalese had not enough to feed their own people and so they had some plan to send us to the group of Bawa Yeshi but we told them we didn't agree. So, they sent the first group to Tashiling, the second to Paljorling and the third group to Kotre Khola. Then, we were ordered to go to Dhuligaunda [= Nepali village near the Jampaling settlement]. When we reached that area, we said we would never go with Bawa Yeshi's group and when the last group was arriving, we stopped the bus by lying on the ground. Later, everybody came out of the bus, but we didn't move. Due to this, we settled in this camp [Jampaling] and are still living here today.

In 1960, Bawa Yeshi was a very good person and all the army respected him. While we were struggling hard and had no food, only one bowl of 'thukpa' [noodle soup] a day, he gave us lectures that he was saving the money for more difficult times. But we didn't know the Lo-Drik-Tsug was receiving money from foreign countries. When we came to know, he was asked to leave and received a promotion in the Tibetan government, and returned to Dharamsala. At that time, I heard from someone that he carried his belongings and bags of money with him on twenty to thirty horses. Gen Wangdu told us: "No matter what he carries, let him go". But some of the group made a plan to beat him, unfortunately this plan was leaked and Bawa Yeshi ran away and settled in Kathmandu. There he had contacts with the secretary of the Nepalese Home Minister and spent a lot of money on this man. He planned to give all the Lo-Drik-Tsug's money to the Ministry. He was bluffing a lot. When we were in Nuwakot, someone came to us and told us we could join their group because they had lots of money.

This is only a small part of my story, if I tell you my entire story, you will need so many days…

ADVICE TO THE YOUNGER GENERATION

I advice them to study very hard and to do research about what we did and follow the advice of the Dalai Lama who always stresses on education. So you have to get good education; for the sake of our country every youth must have a good knowledge.

Interview conducted on 13 June 2007 in Jampaling.

Lundhup Gyaltsen

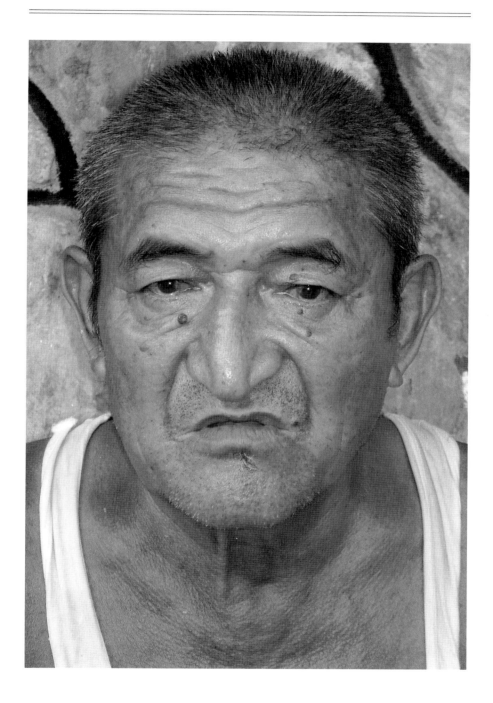

He is also a friend of Lhundup Tsondu and born in the same place. He passed away in 2009.

I am 67 years old and I was born in Jhang in U-Tsang. My father's name was Jigme and my mother's name was Sonam Lhamo. I had eleven brothers and sisters and I was the youngest. Right now I don't know if they are still alive or not, I lost contact. My family was very rich: we were farmers, but we also had many yaks and did business. In summertime we sold yak skin, wool, cheese and butter. I was too young to do business with the family, but my elder brothers did. They brought salt to the village and exchanged it for sheep and tsampa. When I was young, I became monk.

When I was eighteen, I escaped from Tibet together with forty monks and Rinpoche Jampa Khedup of our Monastery. Also your father, Lhundup Tsondu [he is speaking to the Tibetan girl who is interviewing him] was along with me, he was the youngest. We were always good friends and we rode horses together. Before we escaped, we fought the Chinese. They did lots of violations and beat Tibetans and monks and we also beat them. Some of us wore the protective amulet and the bullets didn't hit our body. That time Kelsang's horse was badly hurt and Kelsang, Rinpoche's brother, was hurt too at his leg. Due to this injury, the horse died afterwards.

When we reached the north part of Tibet, Jhang, the Chinese fired at us and killed lots of our animals. Also one person named Khyenrab, his horse was killed by the Chinese. On the way we got lots of problems of food and water. When we reached Mustang we also had food problems so we asked some people food and clothes. With Lhundup Tsondu and a Khampa man, I don't remember his name, we were looking for food; since there were no Chinese, it was easy to go around and ask it to the people. Ten days after I reached Mustang, I heard the news about the flight of the Dalai Lama; we were so happy. If the Dalai Lama would not have been alive, we would be nothing and Tibet would be lost. In 1959, when I reached Mustang, I was nineteen years old and later we reached Yarabug; there we started a military base, so people coming from different parts of Tibet joined.

In the beginning we had a very difficult time to get food and have everything organised. Later, when we got the financial support of the American government, our situation improved. I was not in training in US but some leaders were sent for training. Everybody who went there had a degree, but I never studied. I like to drink; in fact I drink a lot. I don't remember that much, but when I was in Mustang, it was the most difficult time in my life.

Bawa Yeshi was the leader of the Lo-Drik-Tsug organisation. Due to the conflict that took place between Gadon Wangdu and him, the situation became too difficult. But I don't know much about it.

ADVICE TO THE YOUNGER GENERATION

I have not much advice to give to the youngsters, only that they have to learn how to fight the Chinese and join the army. I have no education so people will not listen to me, I am nothing.

Interview conducted on 2 July 2007 in Jampaling.

Bado

During the interview, he was very absent-minded.

I am 76 years old and I was born in Nangchen in Kham. My father's name was Tsega whereas my mother's name was Chukyi. In my family there were three boys. Since we were very poor, we were servants of people and received money from them.

In Tibet, I saw many atrocities done by the Chinese; they killed many Tibetans and I was put in jail for three months. When I lived in jail in Dompa, the Chinese asked me where my Lama was. They told me I had to bring him to my side; but I told them he had fled from the monastery.

The storeroom of the monastery was filled with gold, knifes and guns given by people when they died, and also a lot of butter, cheese and tsampa. The Chinese set fire to everything. They made us destroy the big utensils [metal containers] which were used to make tea for the monks. They caught all the monks. In prison we were with 200 to 300 people. Sometimes the Chinese made us work very hard, mostly we had to clean the toilets and the horse stables; they didn't beat me, but kept on asking where the Lama was. I told them that since I came from a very poor family, I hadn't had the chance to see him. After I left from jail, I met my Lama and my brother in Tilyag gompa in Nangchen and when my brother died, I joined the army.

I joined the Lo-Drik-Tsug in Mustang, I don't know exactly the year but it was at the same time as my friend Tsondu [in 1960]. I joined this organisation to kill the enemies, the Chinese, and to live our own life in Tibet, so that the Dalai Lama and the Tibetans could live united.

I haven't been for training in the US, I got training in Mustang. At that time, we were 1,500 soldiers. Each group had a teacher, namely the thirty people who got training in the US. I remember the things we were doing, we did study of army training and sometimes we worked in the field.

Bawa Yeshi was a leader of the Lo-Drik-Tsug. There was a conflict between some leaders and him because he stole the money given by the American government. It gave lots of sufferings for the soldiers.

I always think of the Chinese who had done bad policy towards us. So I think that, if I get the chance to fight them, I am still ready to do it.

ADVICE TO THE YOUNGER GENERATION

You, the youngsters have to think to study hard and rule the country. According to the Dalai Lama, you are the future generation of the country, so you also have to study hard and do good deeds. Don't steal things, do not tell lies and be a man of good character. You are like a seed from a flower, so you must think you have a country and you have to put the seed in the country and the flower will grow. So you have to get it back.

Interview conducted on 16 June 2007 in Jampaling.

Kunga Chime

I am 75 years old and I was born in Nangchen in Kham. My father's name was Buga and my mother's name was Tsering Lhamo. I had two sisters. Our occupation was agriculture and nomad.

I saw lots of the atrocities, the Chinese killed many Tibetans and also I don't know whether my family is still alive or if they died during that war. When I was twenty-seven years old, I joined the Chushi Gangdruk in 1957. I was member of the group that was living in Tsetang. There we have been fighting the Chinese, that's why I didn't know what happened in Norbulingka. And also there I heard the Dalai Lama already escaped from Norbulingka to India. Then in Lhoka there were getting more Chinese soldiers, so we couldn't face them and that's why we also escaped to India.

I was twenty-eight when we were in Misamari. For nearly one year we have been working in the road construction, it was very hard work and also very hot. Every day people died due to the heat.

Then, the Tibetan government sent me to Mustang and the first year we had a very difficult life there, especially we had not enough to eat. Afterwards it was getting better and better but I don't know how it came; maybe we got support from foreigners. Some of the Tibetans got training from western countries and they trained us how to use guns and how to read a map. A few times, I went into Tibet for guerrilla fighting but I didn't meet any Chinese so I had no chance to fight them while I was in Mustang.

First, Bawa Yeshi was the main leader of our organisation, then later Gen Wangdu became our leader; then there were some problems but again I don't know what happened.

When I was forty-seven, I came to Paljorling; at that time there wasn't really a good accommodation but now everything is very good. I don't have any family here. In the beginning it was difficult to communicate with the people here and we suffered a lot from TB, lots of people died from TB. So we got medicines and also injections, all for free.

ADVICE TO THE YOUNGER GENERATION

I have no education, so it's very difficult to give any advice, but it's all the same; the Tibetan government has so many documents, people have to learn from there.

Interview conducted on 20 June 2007 in Paljorling.

Kelsang Tsering

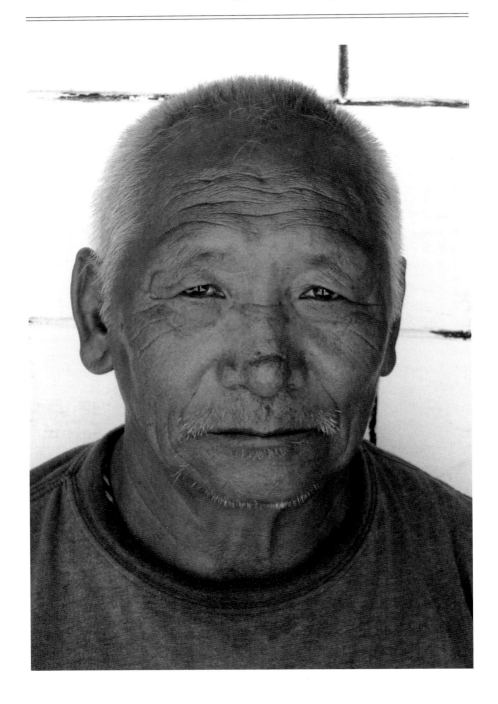

A sense of sadness emanated from him.

I am 74 years old and I was born in Dho-Dupte, a small village near Draktsa in U-Tsang. My father's name was Edog whereas my mother's name was Karma Choezin. We were six in my family: my father, two mothers, two sisters and me; we were nomads.

In the beginning the Chinese were very friendly, they were laughing and looked nice, but later they became very cruel and cunning. They started to threat Tibetans with gun points and made a lot of problems to us, that was the reason why we revolted against them and why the Chushi Gangdruk started. I heard what happened in Eastern Tibet: they interfered in our religious practices and we were not free to live in our own land, we couldn't do what we liked. As soon as I came to know these Chinese policies and due to the fact there was no peace in my country, I joined the Chushi Gangdruk in early 1954 [this organisation only started in 1958] while I was in Tibet. At that time, there were two army cantonments in Lhoka and almost 1,000 soldiers. One group was sent to Kham with Andrug Gompo Tashi and a much bigger group stayed in Lhoka. We fought the Chinese who had an army cantonment in Tsetang. That time, due to the lack of arms and ammunition, we were defeated and so many courageous people who went with their daggers in front of the Chinese, were fired by them. For ten soldiers there was only one gun, some had hand grenades. The fighting took place in Gangbug, an army cantonment near Tsetang. It was very difficult to find Chinese at that time, because they were all hiding in the trenches, so many of our soldiers were killed. After the arrival of a Chinese reinforcement, we were not able to stop them and we fled to India.

WEAPONS FROM THE SKY

First, I reached Montawang, then Misamari and from there I was sent in a group to Sikkim for road construction. There was some plan from the Tibetan government to send some men to Mustang. Later I joined this group and joined the Lo-Drik-Tsug organisation. On the way from Sikkim to Mustang we first reached Tukuche, then we reached Nara Dzong where we lived for almost six or seven months. Then, we reached Shurdig and there was no accommodation, only some tents.[1] I was not in a tent, so with my group we cut juniper and piled it up and made a shelter for us.

I was not in the group that went for training to the US, but I got a military training in Mustang. We had only army training and no other job, we only had to be a soldier. At that time, very few of us had real guns. We were also taught techniques of raid and ambush.

Then we were sent to Yarabug to do training day and night. Afterwards, we were sent to another place, I don't remember the name of that place. Once we were told that behind the mountains there were arms, but that there were also Chinese that we had to face and fight. We had no weapons or ammunition, so we went with only our belongings, swords and daggers, and some old guns to the mountain pass. When we reached behind that mountain, during night-time one airplane circled around and vanished away the first time, at the second round the airplane dropped ammunition and guns and other material. We collected all this and returned. Sometimes I went to the Tibet border to fight the Chinese, but it was never face to face.

I don't want to say many things about Bawa Yeshi. I heard he did corruption of the soldiers' salary and that later there was a lot of internal quarrel among them.

I am thinking of having lost our country and the difficult experience when I arrived in Mustang that we had not enough food to eat or no clothes and we had a great hardship, but my morale was not down, because the challenge motivated my mind. And I was very sad when the Nepalese government came and we had to surrender, this was a very sad moment for me.

I was in Mustang till 1974. We were sent to Nuwakot, a famous jail in Nepal. In Nuwakot some of Bawa Yeshi's group were making propaganda to split the group. We were surrounded by Nepalese soldiers, but we were allowed to go out for one day and could go on our own after taking permission.

Kelsang Tsering looking over the wall during Gonchoe's interview.

When I went to 'Tenshug', I met the Dalai Lama and he made a speech. First he asked: "Who among you were among the first soldiers in Drikuthang where the Chushi Gangdruk was founded?" I was among them and he gave us the advice: "So far your sins are washed away; so from today you should not do any sin and stop eating meat and killing animals".

ADVICE TO THE YOUNGER GENERATION

You should study hard and fight against the Chinese in the same way as we did and you have to liberate Tibet; if it's not whole Tibet, then at least the Tibetan Autonomous Region according to the Dalai Lama's wishes.

Interview conducted on 23 June 2007 in Jampaling.

Lobsang Monlam

If I have to tell you my whole story, it will take at least five to six days; it's much too long. I am 81 years old and I was born in Chungpo area and lived in Rongpo; it's in Kham. My father's name was Dhondup and my mother's name was Pelkar. Our occupation in Tibet was farming and salt business. In 1984 my brothers and sister insisted to come and visit my home in Tibet, then I came to know what happened to my family. Before we had 500 female yaks, 15 horses, 500 sheep and 1,000 goats. I found out all were taken away by the Chinese. This happened not only to our family but also to our neighbours.

When I was three years old, I became a monk till I was thirty-five, so I know what we possessed in the monastery.

Even in our monastery there were lots of ravages; before we had such precious books: the Kangyur and Tengyur and [books of] Je Tsongkhapa [a famous teacher of Buddhism]; they were all burned by the Chinese.[1] Lots of golden statues were all taken away by the Chinese. In this monastery there used to live 500 monks, in 1984 only thirty were left, but most of them became mad, deaf or blind due to the Chinese atrocities.

The Chinese killed two of my brothers together with my uncle who was a high leader of a group of nine villages. They also killed my Lama. In 1949, they came to my village and established a shop, but seventy-five monks of our monastery destroyed this shop.

GOLDEN THRONE

Around 1955, the Chinese came to Lhasa to occupy the city; Andrug Gompo Tashi was the leader and told the people that the Chinese already occupied Lhasa with 40,000 soldiers and that afterwards they would kill the Dalai Lama. He suggested that since the Dalai Lama was young, we would do 'Tenshug' and give him a golden throne; and then we started secretly because some members of the Chushi Gangdruk had connections with the Chinese and we had to keep our plan secret. People from Kham and Amdo supported his idea and started making this throne. It's main goal was to gather people against the Chinese. It was a very difficult time because higher Tibetan officers, thirty monks and thirty lay people collaborated with the Chinese. Each of them received 3,000 or 4,000 ngul-dayen a month, depending on their capacities and level.[2] That time, only people from Kham and Amdo, especially the Chushi Gangdruk, opposed the Chinese.

In 1956 we finished the golden throne and offered 'Tenshug'; at that time thousands of people attended the celebration, so the Chushi Gangdruk got the chance to say *'Tashi Delek'* to the Dalai Lama. He was only sixteen years old and took the full responsibility of the country. It was really a hard time to organise everything, because nobody was allowed to enter his palace, except for one person, Pala Thupten [his chamberlain].

Chushi Gangdruk sent a message through him to ask the Dalai Lama if the best place to establish the army camp was either north or south. He replied we'd best go south. Then everybody went south, there were almost 1,000 soldiers. Among them, leaders were selected and three different groups were made. One group had to go to Norbulingka to protect the Dalai Lama; the second group went to protect the area of Kongpo, Yalung and Tsetang and the third group, including me and Gompo Tashi went to the north to Powo Tamo, it was the main way used by the Chinese to enter Tibet. That place is bare land: there was no food, not even water. We reached Moishung hill, so we were clever and went around this hill but we didn't know if there were Chinese at the other side. So, suddenly they bombed us and fifteen to twenty of our soldiers were killed but we also killed lots of them. Our leader Gompo Tashi was badly hurt and bleeding a lot, but still he was courageous and told us we had to go to the other side of the hill because otherwise the Dalai Lama wouldn't be able to pass. We really did hard work and we left Andrug Gompo Tashi in Chakra Palbar. The other soldiers moved to Powo Tamo to block the way for the Chinese. That time a battle took place between the Chinese and our soldiers. Some of ours died but also some Chinese soldiers were killed by us. But if we killed 100 Chinese soldiers, the next day there were 1,000 of them and if we killed 1,000 Chinese, then 10,000 would come.

HELPING TO ESCAPE

So since it was very hard to fight them, we postponed the battle and we felt it was better to help the Dalai Lama to escape from Lhasa. Then we went straight to Lhasa. From there, some of the soldiers including me came with him to Lhoka and then to India. When he entered India, we returned to Lhoka and we protected some ordinary Tibetans, who were escaping to India, against the Chinese troops. Almost 10 to 20,000 Tibetan people could escape to India thanks to our support and protection. Since it was really impossible to continue to fight the Chinese, we also decided to escape to India. We arrived in Montawang and on reaching the border the police took all our weapons. Then we reached Misamari where the climate was too hot, you really didn't need any clothes.

When I was in Tibet fighting the Chinese, one bullet hit my leg, but I didn't feel any pain; being in India, it became worse. Today, there is still a little difference between my legs. It was really unbelievable, without any 'Tso Sung' from the Dalai Lama or from Pempa Rinpoche, each Tibetan soldier would have been riddled by thousands of Chinese bullets. I got these protective amulets when I was in Tibet, and I got other precious blessings. The Chinese used to say that these splitting people were like stones, we cannot kill them, unless we fight them face to face and one Tibetan for ten Chinese. But some of our soldiers who didn't keep their body clean, maybe they were killed by the Chinese even if they wore 'Tso Sung'?

In 1959, I was in Misamari, it was really impossible to live there, you died due to the hot climate. So, we asked the Indian government to send us to another place; we were sent to Bomdila for road construction, only for two or three months. There we also had a very hard life. So, every day four to five people escaped from there. Then we had a meeting and discussed that our country was in Chinese hands, our family and brothers were killed by the Chinese and now we were working here in India in road construction, so it had really no sense, so we decided to migrate to Mustang to fight the Chinese. It didn't matter if we could get back our country from the Chinese or if we could only kill one or two Chinese, at least that was already something. Then we went to Mustang. There were fifteen groups; I belonged to the third group. We had so many different responsibilities, so I was leader of twenty soldiers and also of those who were spying. I stayed in Mustang for fifteen years.

"MONEY MAKES MAN CRAZY"

My experience is that all over the world you should not follow the path of money, because it makes man crazy. Due to some of the higher people of Tibet who were corrupted by money, our country was captured by the Chinese. Never trust the Chinese, because when they want something, they will spend lots of money to obtain it.

[laughing] I am a little bit shy to explain about Bawa Yeshi. He was the chief leader selected by Andrug Gompo Tashi, but he didn't listen to his orders since Gompo Tashi stayed in India. Usually the Tibetan government had counted [food and supplies] for 500 soldiers, but we were 1,500 soldiers, so we suffered from lack of food and cold. Anyway, Bawa Yeshi corrupted our salary for fifteen years. He took all the salary to Nepal and afterwards he surrendered to the Nepalese government. We also gave our weapons to the Nepalese government and then we were sent to Nuwakot jail; actually it is the ninth worst prison in Nepal [he meant to say this jail was not so bad since they were guarded in an open area]. They didn't give us any punishment, but at night we heard the prisoners screaming, so we believed they killed those who were sentenced to death. We stayed there for six months, and then reached Jampaling.

ADVICE TO THE YOUNGER GENERATION

All the younger Tibetans have to take the opportunity to learn the Tibetan culture and traditions, and the Tibetan way of living while we, the old people, are still alive. If the elders die, the younger ones will not get any knowledge about Tibet. If we get the chance to go back to Tibet, there are lots of provinces where the Tibetan lifestyle is mostly nomadic and farming, so they have to know how to do this work. We cannot always depend on the western countries to get a sponsorship, so when we get freedom, we have to stand on our own feet and use our own hands.

Interview conducted on 1 July 2007 in Jampaling.

Dhukar

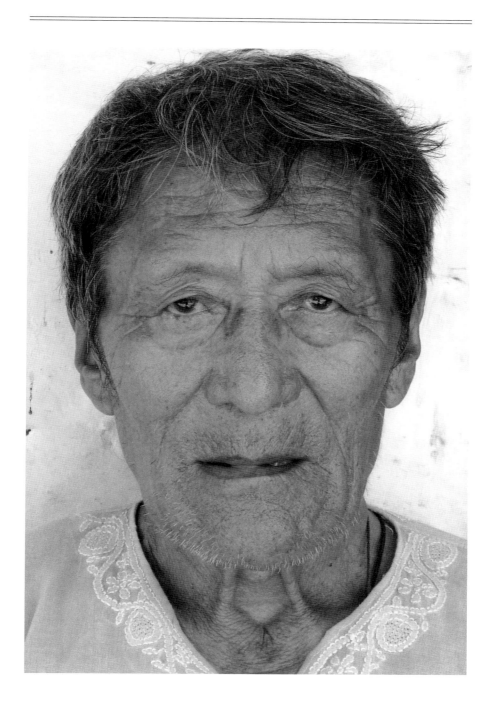

I am 79 years old and I was born in Derge Deckyi Ling Tsang in Kham. My father's name was Choephel whereas my mother's was Choenya Lhamo. I had one brother and my parents, who passed away in Tibet. Our occupation in Tibet was both working in the field and rearing domestic animals like nomads.

I don't want to tell you many things, because it was so much suffering that we underwent. We offered our life for our nation, but it was our duty, so there is nothing to tell. If I tell all my story, I could tell you many stories, but it's better to be short.

BEATEN ONE BY ONE

I left my home in 1958, and for one year I fought against the Chinese as a civil. I saw a lot of atrocities, that I am not able to tell you in short. They have been killing so many people and destroying the monasteries and so on. They were killing especially rich people and leaders. Ordinary Tibetans were forced by them to beat their superiors or aristocrats. It's hard to imagine all these cruelties, but they are still in my mind.

When the Chinese beat the Tibetans, they all had to stand in a line and the rich people and the higher people were beaten one by one; they fell down, but I don't know what happened to them, if afterwards they died or not …

When I came from Tibet, I was not a soldier, just a layman and the Chinese had killed all my family members. In 1959, I escaped from Tsang to Mustang and then to India. I was not with those who followed a training in America and I was not with the Dalai Lama when he escaped to India, since I escaped from the other side of Tibet. I went from Kham to Siling then to Golok Machin [in Amdo], Tsang and from there to Mustang and finally to India. In Bodh Gaya, I met the Dalai Lama and I got an audience with him. I gave my name to join the Chushi Gangdruk. After that, we went to Kalimpong in Sikkim and shifted to Gangtok afterwards.

I went to Mustang in 1960 where we fought like guerrillas. If I tell you about the living conditions of the Chushi Gangdruk, they were very poor as, I'm sure, the other retired soldiers must have told you explicitly. If I tell you about the guerrilla, we could only think of how to kill the Chinese and we were not thinking about food. We didn't have much experience as modern soldiers, we were only learning guerrilla fighting to annoy the Chinese. We were fighting on and off and doing exercises. Sometimes due to the lack of weapons, we carved wood to console ourselves as it looked like we were carrying a real weapon.

There were so many leaders, but most of them already died. I just give you a few names: Pedho, Njarung Kelsang Dorjee, Ragra, Tsering Dorjee …

Bawa Yeshi was a member of the other group, so we were not connected. Officially I was not a member of their group, so I don't know much about him and his group.

I could tell you stories for two days, but it's almost the same as the others and since you are interviewing them all...

ADVICE TO THE YOUNGER GENERATION

I already decided when I was young, that I would offer my life to the nation, that's why there was nothing to think about myself, no selfishness. I have always been determined to do and die from the time I joined the army and still that strong determination rings in my heart. For the advice, I am not the best man, I don't know anything, so I cannot advice the younger generation; but if I were still strong and had more experience, I could be the leader of the younger generation against China, but I am old now. So everybody has to think about life in our country, then you know the need for dedication to our country in difficult times.

Interview conducted on 11 June 2007 in Jampaling.

Tsering Dhondup

I am 77 years old and I was born in 1931 in a place called Toe-Saga-Dzong, which is in U-Tsang. My father's name was Chorpo whereas my mother's name was Lhadon. I had two brothers and three sisters in my family, who later on all lived their own life. Our main occupation was nomad: we sold 'tsepa' [yak hair] to make tents and sheep wool to make mattresses and clothes and we did big business. We milked the 'dri', sometimes we drunk the milk ourselves, sometimes we sold it. We also made butter and cheese. Some of my brothers and sisters stayed nomad, while others went to the north to collect salt and exchange it for grains.

The Chinese came to Tibet in 1956 from the border of Kham and then later in 1958, they went to Lhasa and due to that the Dalai Lama was forced to leave to a foreign country. Tibet has been very peaceful for so many years and was not interested in army and ammunition and not used to violence, but then the Chinese came and they were more powerful and some people started to leave the country, some of them stayed inside [Tibet] and faced lots of problems. Since we couldn't live like this, for that aim we had the spirit to regain our country. We didn't have any arms or weapons and we couldn't fight the Chinese. Some of us had the spirit of coming in exile and had the aim of joining the Chushi Gangdruk.

I have seen some public 'thamzings' in Tibet. The Chinese were saying that lots of reactionaries had the intention to go to a foreign country. "If you also go, then you too will face problems and anyway, finally you will come under our hand". I was also arrested by them and the Chinese were talking to us like that. We were thirty to forty people and we were kept for two or three days in a stable and guarded by the Chinese army. Afterwards the Chinese left and we were released without any reason.

I have also seen lots of monasteries being destroyed, e.g. in my village, the monastery named Dhargyling was totally destroyed. All the sacred prayer books were taken out and were used to make mattresses or chairs; from the cloth covering of these books were made women clothes like trousers and jackets. They put some mani stones inscribed with sacred mantras and the books on the streets and made people dance on them. My uncle, who was the leader of our village was especially handled roughly; they told him he was rich before, and that now he would be poor. The Chinese forced the poor villagers to beat him and he was killed before my eyes.

A LOT OF HARDSHIP

I escaped three months after the Dalai Lama; while he took the road to Bomdila and Gangtok, I took the road from Toe to India. I came to India as a refugee and afterwards I joined the Chushi Gangdruk in Mustang in 1960. We stayed in Nepal and fought the Chinese in Tibet. In the Chushi Gangdruk, we had to work very hard, we stayed in the mountains, had not enough food nor clothes, we faced a lot of hardship. And we did guerrilla war from there into Tibet and back to our station in Nepal; it was very difficult. After these difficulties, we were still continuing. If we went into

Tibet, there were Chinese, in Mustang there were Nepalese. We were mainly staying in a defensive position, sometimes we attacked.

When I look back, I am still remembering the bad condition in Tibet and the suffering and lack of food and clothes in Mustang. But in spite of all this suffering, I am still dreaming of regaining Tibet. Because I still hope that due to the Dalai Lama's kindness and the international support for the Tibetan justice issue, he will get back Tibet before he dies.

The experience in Mustang was really bitter, we were staying in a very remote area, but we did this for our country. Our kaki tents were picked in the mountains and trenches dug all around. For two or three hours we had to keep vigil from the top of the hill or from the trench to see if the Chinese were coming; and if they were, we had to report this. Our tents were completely worn-out. We didn't have good clothes, since we couldn't go to the village or to the market to buy new ones. All day we were wearing this kaki chuba. In Mustang we had no other choice than bear this suffering to have a better future for Tibet.

When we were in Mustang, Bawa Yeshi was the leader of our camp. Afterwards he didn't do the right thing, he was only favouring his country-men [from Kham]. He was not paying regularly our monthly salary and that demoralized the troops. What hard labour we had given, it didn't bear fruit.

ADVICE TO THE YOUNGER GENERATION

For example, my parents' generation has passed away and my generation is also nearly at the end of our lives and now the present generation gets a good education like you [pointing to the young interviewer] and as the Dalai Lama says: "Tibet is a good cause and you should defend this cause through dialogue." The future generation has to keep Tibet independent and has to know the Tibetan history. That is the main thing and our generation is handing this to you and you have to continue. I also feel very happy about the twenty-first century and the education you are receiving and that you are doing well.

I have no advice to give, because there is the Dalai Lama and the government, they have their point of view and you should follow this. My personal advice is that the younger generation should follow good things and keep the Tibetan identity. You see, Tibet is a beautiful country with pure air, clean water, there are several species and good water and in Tibet we never had these kind of sicknesses like TB; I had never heard of it during my life in Tibet. I explain these things to the younger generation and even to my children.

I am not the leader, I don't have much experience to give a speech.

Interview conducted on 11 June 2007 in Jampaling.

Tashi Dorjee

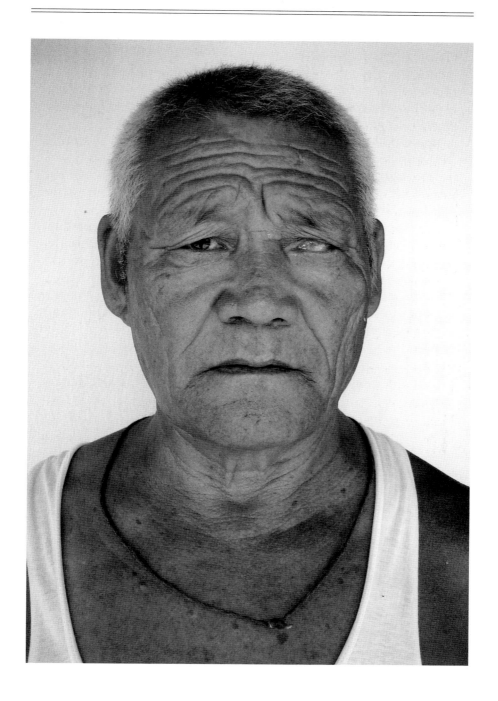

I am 67 years old and I was born in Toe Choekhor in U-Tsang. My father's name was Pema Wangdak and my mother's name was Khado. In my family there were eight members: three brothers, two sisters, my parents and me; we were nomads.

I joined the soldiers of the Chushi Gangdruk in 1962 in Mustang. I was doing some household job in somebody's home when I heard about this organisation and I had to join. After my mother had died from a natural cause and my father was killed by the Chinese, I was taken by the Chinese to graze the animals and had to do some forced labour. I cannot remember so much about the earlier times in Tibet, only that I was grazing the animals when I was thirteen years old.

My experience with the Lo-Drik-Tsug was rearing cattle, I also have not much memories about it. [laughing] The high placed persons, the leaders had their own future plans, their real work was not known by the ordinary soldiers and sometimes they had a quarrel. Bawa Yeshi did corruption of the soldiers' salary.

[Since the man has one damaged eye, I asked him when this happened.] It happened in Mustang in 1965; I was an assistant cook and one day when I was chopping the wood for the cooking, I broke the wood on my knee and the branch hit my eye.

I was not in a US training camp, because at that time I was in Mustang working as a servant. And I didn't accompany the Dalai Lama since I left after him, but I heard about his flight when I had reached Mustang.

When I went to 'Tenshug', the Dalai Lama asked me some questions: "Where are you from and what are doing now?" Only these questions, because around 100 people were there, so there were not much questions for each.

ADVICE TO THE YOUNGER GENERATION

You have to study hard and follow the advice of the Dalai Lama and do something for your own country.

Interview conducted on 17 June 2007 in Jampaling.

Tashi Choempel

My name is Tashi Choempel, but they call me Gara Guduk. I am 70 years old and I was born in Tadun in the area of Ngari in U-Tsang. My father's name was Tsering Topgyal whereas my mother's name was Yanchen Dolkar. In my family we were six: my father and mother and four boys, I was the eldest. Our occupation was nomad.

I think I left Tibet when I was twenty years old. I don't know the exact age, but I joined the Chushi Gangdruk when I was thirty. At that time, they were already active in Mustang.

I was a member but not a fighter, I was the cook of Bawa Gen Yeshi and his group. Most of the time I was cooking for ten to fifteen people but sometimes there was some special meeting and then there were around twenty.

I don't know clearly what Bawa Yeshi has done with the money sent by the CIA, I was only a cook. If I had worked in the office, I would have known. I didn't see him put money in his own pocket but afterwards some people were telling this but they didn't like him and made up this story. I really don't know what happened.

I have no important things to tell. At the end, everybody gave the weapons to the Nepalese government; I felt very sad, because I couldn't do anything else but do the same.

SAD TO DIE HERE

If Tibet becomes free, then I want to go back, otherwise I will die in Nepal, but I will be pretty sad [he starts laughing]. It's difficult to fight the Chinese because now I am becoming old, but if I got the opportunity to fight them, I would still do it.

When I was in this Chushi Gangdruk organisation, I could fight them and try to get back the country and go back, but if we don't succeed to get the country back, I feel that I will die here in Nepal.

ADVICE TO THE YOUNGER GENERATION

I had never the opportunity to have education in Tibet, I was a servant all my life, so I cannot give any advice. But the young people have so much opportunities, so don't miss the opportunity to study, to become a good person, to have respect for other people, for the nation and the elders. It's your responsibility to take our motherland back and to win our freedom back.

Interview conducted on 8 June 2007 in Jampaling.

Norbu Dorjee

From 1975 till November 2007, he was the camp leader of the Paljorling refugee camp in Pokhara.

I am 65 years old and I was born in Dartsedo in Kham. My father's name was Tsering Dhondup and my mother's name Yama Khando. I had three brothers and one sister. Two of my brothers died in Tibet and one brother came here in Paljorling. My sister is still living in Tibet, in Lhasa. She invited me to visit her, but I have no time. I never returned back. Our occupation was doing business and agriculture. We exchanged salt for tea. When we were in India, we were doing the clothes' business and exchanged them for Tibetan woolen items.

UPRISING IN LHASA

When I was in Tibet, I joined the Chushi Gangdruk, it was around 1957, and in 1959, I was in Lhasa. We protected the Dalai Lama; lots of people from Kham, Amdo, from everywhere, not only from Lhasa gathered and were revolting against the Chinese. The reason for the gathering was that the Chinese had come to some regions saying they wanted to develop Tibet and that when it was developed, they would go back to China and leave Tibet to the Tibetans. But after some time the situation became worse: there are many fields in Tibet and they were taking more and more taxes from the farmers; also people had to give them their weapons and horses. They forced the poor people to rob the rich ones and after having given it to the government, it was divided equally among all the people. They started a propaganda campaign for communism and they were saying that insects attack rotten meat. They compared the Dalai Lama with the rotten meat; saying that if this rotten meat was removed, the insects would not attack the meat anymore.

Then, one day the Chinese invited the Dalai Lama by sending him a letter to attend a program in their army camp. That time we were young and common people from Lhasa and other regions wanted to speak to the Tibetan administration and tell them the Dalai Lama should not go to the Chinese dinner. Some members of the public and some officials leaders were discussing and decided the Dalai Lama should not go. Immediately all the people from Lhasa and other regions of Tibet gathered at Norbulingka and surrounded the summer palace. We had brought our own food and weapons with us. Then the soldiers from Kham with guns and horses were divided into north, south, east, west, different sides of Norbulingka. Other Tibetan soldiers were not there, only people from Lhasa and business people from other regions.

The Chinese were already present in Lhasa; most of the important areas were captured by them. They sent a message to the officials and the guerrillas that they were going to shoot the Norbulingka area and kill the Dalai Lama. I only heard it from the Tibetan officials, so we had to be careful. After that news, some officials and Chushi Gangdruk armed soldiers secretly left Norbulingka area in the late night to come in exile. The Dalai Lama left Norbulingka, without taking off his lama dress and just wearing a Tibetan chuba on top of it, so that nobody could recognize him. So, he escaped that night and had to flee from Tibet. Three days later, he reached Lhoka and then the Chinese started to attack Norbulingka. In the Lhoka area the Tibetan army and the Chushi Gangdruk protected the Dalai Lama.

In Lhasa, I didn't know where the Chinese were hiding on the hill side. They used a big gun-fire on Norbulingka. First, they started with guns and later on, more violently with gun-fire and other missile guns. First, we heard the gunfire, later the explosions of bombs, bang, bang.

Actually Norbulingka is a beautiful place like to go for picnic. You will not see such a beautiful place in another area of Tibet; but beautiful birds dropped to the ground due to the toxic smoke, and also dogs turned around and fell down. I could see nothing else, there was only the booming of guns [explains this very expressively while gesturing his hands]. In Norbulingka, I saw lots of dead men and horses and trees were falling down on the way, so it was very hard to pass. So, we decided not to stay there and we crossed a big river nearby.

HIT BY A CHINESE BULLET

I had three friends with me and we only had one small and one big gun. We tried to cross this river by horse, but the Chinese were shooting at us and my horse and my friend's horse were killed. Our horses were carrying loads and some food, so we had to take everything by ourselves and had to cross on foot. At that time, thousands of people were crossing the river and running away. After having crossed the river, I was sitting on a rock and was shooting the Chinese but I couldn't see them. Later a Chinese bullet hit me in the back. If you want to see it, I can show you. It was difficult to continue but I didn't suffer too much. We still continued to run away; later I got problems to move and so I took off all my clothes and I pulled out the bullet. After that, it was very hard to go on, but one of my best friends was dying, so I stayed with him and tears came from his eyes, and I was crying too. He told me since he couldn't move from there, that instead of staying, me and my other friend should leave.

It was very amazing because I wore a yellow shirt and 'gawu', and although the Chinese were continuously shooting at me and the bullets were flying about our ears, we never got injured thanks to the protection of 'gawu'.

After reaching the hill, I couldn't walk anymore, I didn't meet any people there and so I went to sleep since I felt completely exhausted. I thought that if the Chinese would have arrived then, they could kill me; I didn't care.

Then later, one of my friends came to me with a horse that was not killed by the Chinese. When he saw me, he felt very sad and put me on his horse. After one and a half day, we reached the Chushi Gangdruk army camp. There were some Tibetan doctors, who had studied in India and returned to Tibet. There stayed about thirty to forty injured patients in the hospital and I remained there for more than one month. One bullet was still under my skin and when the doctor started to take it out, I fell totally unconscious. After one month, I felt better. Again, the Chinese came to this area, and were still attacking but that time we were in the lower part of Tibet and we ran away and continued to walk and finally reached the Indian border. Then, we stayed in Misamari for more than one month.

TRAINING IN THE US & MUSTANG

It's such a long story. In 1960, 2,000 soldiers were sent to Mustang. From this group some people went for training to the US, I also went from 1959 and came back to Mustang in 1960. There were different groups, and among the groups fifteen soldiers were chosen by the Chushi Gangdruk leaders: Gompo Tashi and Jampa Gyatso, so it was not our own choice to be sent. When we were selected, they asked us individually if we wanted to go for training for the sake of the country. I agreed because I wanted to go. I struggled a lot for the Lo-Drik-Tsug organisation and I just tell you my short story because if I tell you my whole history, it is too long. So I want to stop here. If you have still any remaining questions to ask me, I am ready to answer.

[Can you give us some more details about the training in the US?]

We were given training by English speaking persons and an English speaking Tibetan translated. There were so many soldiers like me who did not know English. We got training like guerrillas, spy training and we learned about walkie-talkie and all the activities done by the guerrilla force. We studied for one year and some months. In my group there were about twenty to thirty people. I think there was a good atmosphere and we did the training very happily.

[So then you went back to Mustang and gave training to others?]

Yes, we did and we were dropped at night from an airplane with a parachute. We all jumped one by one, some ten to fifteen soldiers. It was nice. Yapooodoo!! [laughing and still enjoying the memory]. When I reached Mustang, I felt very glad because I was almost back in Tibet, but at the same time I was afraid because the Chinese could kill me. All the guerrillas and other friends were waiting to welcome us with a scarf and we didn't get any difficulties to settle.

[Are there any pictures of this period?]

We used to have some pictures, but I am not sure that I still have them [two pictures in the historical background chapter are his].

When we were in Mustang, we did guerrilla actions. We went to Tibet to attack Chinese trucks, we also killed them. Most of the time it was difficult to find where the Chinese were but we were always ready to fight and to attack.

I knew Bawa Yeshi very well, he was a leader of the Lo-Drik-Tsug. First he acted in a very straight way, but later he took the curved way, then he split from the Lo-Drik-Tsug organisation. There is a Tibetan saying: 'First he was a man, afterwards he became a ghost', to indicate someone who is first acting very bravely, making good history, but afterwards he has no principles, kills people, does corruption and makes bad history.

SURRENDER

In 1974, the Nepalese government told the guerrilla forces they were not allowed to stay in Mustang, because it would create a conflict between the Chinese and the Nepalese government. Unfortunately, in 1974 we had so many weapons to give to them. A message came from the Dalai Lama to hand over the weapons to the Nepalese government and not to fight back.

Later, we shifted to Pokhara to the Paljorling camp. The Jampaling settlement was also given by the Nepalese government to one part of the Lo-Drik-Tsug organisation that came from Kotre Khola, a camp which was not given by the Nepalese government, but purchased by ourselves. Lots of Lo-Drik-Tsug soldiers live in Jampaling till now and some of them live here; people could choose where they wanted to live.

So there are four Tibetan camps in Pokhara's valley. So this is the camp which was established quite late in 1974 together with Jampaling, while other camps were established around 1960.

[Anything more to tell?]

No, I have nothing more to tell. If I tell about my life, it will not be finished not only today, but even not tomorrow.

Actually we had a hard life: we left Tibet in 1959, then we fled to India and then from India to Mustang. Mustang lies between the border of Nepal and Tibet. Now those who were in Mustang, they are getting old and have their own family with lots of children. Now I am becoming old, but when I was in Mustang, I was the youngest.

ADVICE TO THE YOUNGER GENERATION

We are always talking about the youngsters' welfare. To make them study hard, we face lots of financial problems, but it is our duty to send them to school. I told my whole story to the youngsters and that our country is in Chinese hands, but I couldn't say them they have to kill the Chinese as the Dalai Lama teaches us that you have to give respect or do prostration to those who are doing bad to you. In this century, we are doing everything for peace.

Interview conducted on 18 June 2007 in Paljorling.

Tashi Phuntsok

I am 67 years old and I was born in Namrik in the north part of Tibet, in U-Tsang. My father's name was Tamdin Wangyal and my mother's name was Rinzin Dolma. My family had eight members: three brothers and me, two sisters and my parents. We were nomads, we made butter and cheese and we could sell it sometimes.

CHEATING THE CHINESE

When I was seventeen, the Chinese started to occupy the whole of Tibet and moved more northwards, so many Tibetans escaped and arrived in Toe. I already felt that they would come very soon to my town and indeed they did; they started to destroy the monastery and the stupa, and kill the people. When I saw the Chinese for the first time, several of them came by horse to my village and then they were becoming more numerous and made so many problems.

At that time, it was such a hard life for me because my parents died and also the Chinese they caught the village people. Once they caught me when I was in Lekshe, but I told them that the next day we had to move to another place as nomads, so I cheated them and I ran away and I left all the yaks, sheep and other animals and all the precious things from my grandparents and I escaped to Toe Jhang. When I escaped, on the way I was a servant in different families. When we were still in Tibet, we heard about the Dalai Lama who fled to India, of course then we also ran away.

Then, I arrived in Mustang and I joined the Chushi Gangdruk in 1963. At that time the living conditions were very poor. Of course I didn't get training in the US because I was in Mustang; those who were sent for training left from Misamari.

I stayed in Mustang as a guerrilla for fourteen years. When I reached the age of twenty-two, I went to Tibet to fight. Two times I was in Chang and one time in Dolpo [border of Nepal], but we didn't meet any Chinese there. I was a soldier, but for two years I looked after the yaks and horses, then for three years, I did some agriculture work and also some small business which was necessary for the army camp: I transported salt from Bhairawa.

Bawa Yeshi was our leader and afterwards he did corruption by taking the soldiers' salary. He did bad things because he killed Tibetans, he is a very bad man, that is all.

ADVICE TO THE YOUNGER GENERATION

I didn't have any education, since I only looked after the animals. The younger generation here really has a good chance to study, so don't waste your time in watching TV or with games or something else.

Interview conducted on 24 June 2007 in Jampaling.

Pema Lhasung

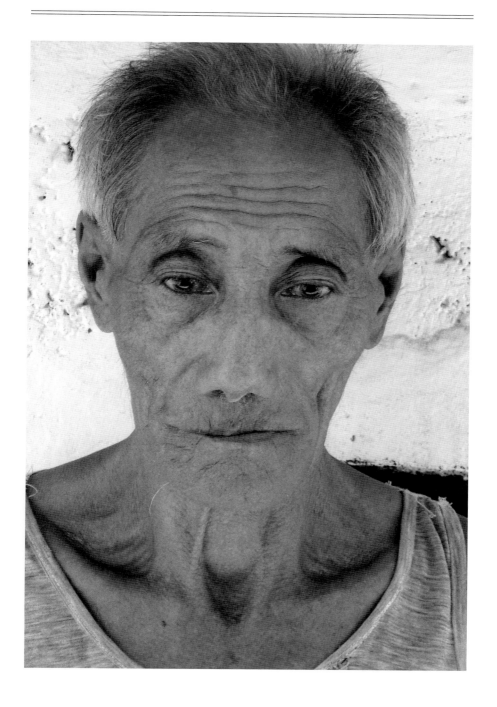

During the interview, he looked very sad; his wife was sitting next to him while turning her prayer wheel around.

I am 77 years old and I was born in Nangchen in Kham. My father's name was Dorga, whereas my mother's name was Gukyi. In my family there were eight members: three brothers and two sisters, and my parents, all were killed by the Chinese except me. Our occupation was only nomad, since in my area there were no farmers.

At that time, they killed a lot of Tibetans in that area and so many Tibetans were killed near the river. The Chinese had long knives and cut the throats and threw the bodies in the river. Each time they killed a group of twenty to thirty. But my parents were killed by a gun. At that time, I was only a young child. They put us in jail for more than two months. But, there was some other problem in China, so the Chinese moved to another place. So me, my uncle and some other people ran away from jail to the north of Tibet, to Toe, and from there to Mustang.

When I reached Mustang, I joined the army of the Chushi Gangdruk because I had seen the Chinese killing all these people and I felt very sad, and had a lot of anger and I tried to take revenge for my family and my country. I stayed there for fourteen years as a guerrilla fighter.

PITY FOR MYSELF

I never had the chance to go to the US for training, but I had a lot of training in Mustang. First, we exercised with wooden weapons, afterwards we got real weapons from the US and we learned how to protect ourselves and how to kill the enemy. This was the first time in my life that I got some education. When I stayed in Mustang, I had to respect the army rules, of course you had not much freedom there. We always were prepared to fight the Chinese and I was very eager to fight them all the time. But such a sad thing happened when the Nepalese government wanted to stop the guerrilla and also the Dalai Lama gave us a message to give all the weapons to the Nepalese and surrender. I was really very angry and I cried. I felt pity for myself because I couldn't take revenge for the murder on my parents. I felt very sad and tears came out. Even now when I am remembering this, tears come out again. And if we had the chance to go back to fight, I really would like to go, but I know my physical condition is not so good, I have a leg problem. I wished I had killed at least one or two Chinese.

I cannot forget my parents were killed by the Chinese and that I had to leave my home and go to Toe where I had a hard time because I was only a servant carrying salt from one village to another. Later, I also was a servant in the region of Mount Kailash; that was really a hard time.

There has been some Long Life praying for the Dalai Lama, but I didn't get the chance to go there because my wife was sick. But before, both of us went a few times to Dharamsala to meet him and he told us to be a good and kind-hearted person.

ADVICE TO THE YOUNGER GENERATION

I really don't know how to give advice, but I told my son what really happened in Tibet and what kind of family we were. We all did some good for our country, even we offered our life for it. So you guys, you have to work hard and study hard and work for our country.

Interview conducted on 17 June 2007 in Jampaling.

Sherap Sangpo

His wife had passed away shortly before the interview; one of his children was listening and questioning him too.

I am 65 years old and I was born in Mangtsa in Toe, the north part of U-Tsang. My father's name was Menga Gowa Tenzin and my mother's name was Khador. In our family we were five: my parents, two boys and one girl. We were nomads.

Since 1959, the Chinese occupied Tibet and in 1960 I came from Tibet to Mustang. In 1962 I returned to Jhang. I had no intention of joining the Chushi Gangdruk because my father had died and my mother was quite old and I wanted to take care of her, but Gen Sonam Tsering came to my place and told me I had to join the organisation because there was an order from the Tibetan government. So I had to join and face battle against the Chinese.

I didn't see any atrocities because when the Chinese were near Mangtsa, we ran away to the border area; it was easy because it only took us one day by horse. My friend Shakpo Gonpo from Amdo accompanied me on my flight, but went back to Jhang to get his cattle. Then he was caught and arrested and sent to jail in Lhasa for five years but we met again here in Nepal. I didn't fight the Chinese in Tibet, but while I stayed in Mustang, I have been fighting them.

Daughter questioning her father.

TEARS IN HIS EYES

My saddest memory is when we were doing guerrilla warfare in Mustang. We didn't declare war, but when the Chinese shot on us, we shot back. In 1971, out of fifty-three horsemen who were fighting the Chinese, some were caught and died; we lost twelve soldiers.

Bawa Yeshi was the leader of the Lo-Drik-Tsug organisation. In the beginning all the leaders were friendly with each other, but he only favoured his own group. Later, when he started the salary corruption, the conflict began between them. The army went to Jhang and they killed animals and we received this meat. Bawa Yeshi also forcibly took the yaks of the villagers without even paying them, but pretending he had bought them with our salary. So we were divided in two groups, I was not in his group. They went to another place and the two groups started fighting and some people were killed.

In Mustang, I never went to school, I only learned the tactics of fighting with guns and guerrilla training.

LIKE ORPHANS

Bawa Yeshi sympathized with the Nepalese government. Gen Wangdu and his group fled for twelve days towards India. At a one day's distance from the border, a spy of Bawa Yeshi made a phone call to inform where they would be the next day and then ran away from the group. This information was passed to Bawa Yeshi and soldiers arrived. Gen Wangdu was standing in the middle of the group of soldiers, then six of them who were in front of him ran away and so he got killed. We felt like orphans when this happened [he has tears in his eyes when telling this], but his body was never found. Gen Wangdu was a very courageous man, he followed the instructions of the Tibetan government and was a true follower of the Dalai Lama. If he hadn't been killed, we wouldn't face so much problems now. For me and my group, it's like a dog's life here. Afterwards, I went to Dharamsala for this Long Life religious performance, which we call 'Tenshug'. The Dalai Lama asked me : "How did you flee from Tibet and during your escape have you met any Chinese?" I answered him: "No, I escaped before the Chinese came, but when I was in Mustang, we were fighting them and then we lost twelve men".

ADVICE TO THE YOUNGER GENERATION

The younger ones have to study and continue to study hard.

Interview conducted on 17 June 2007 in Jampaling.

Kunga

I am 77 years old and I was born in Derge in Kham. My father's name was Kunchok and mother's name was Tsetso. There were four members in my family: I was the only son and I had one sister. But there were many relatives on father's and mother's side. Our occupation in Tibet was doing business in the border area. I was selling some medicines from the Americans to China and also some materials for clothes. When I was two or three years old, there was some fighting in Derge between the villagers and my family wasn't able to stay there and escaped to Lhasa.

I joined the Chushi Gangdruk after the Dalai Lama escaped to India in 1959, at that time the general leader was Kunluwang. I was in Norbulingka, especially people from Derge protected the Dalai Lama there and most of our people were very capable to do security. Next to Kunluwang, there were also some other high officers as leaders of the Chushi Gangdruk and security people. At that time in Lhasa, there were so many security people, as well from Chinese as from Tibetan side. We tried to do security and help the Dalai Lama to escape,

Kunga, 25 years old in 1955.

so our Derge people stayed in the south gate of Norbulingka, that is the main gate from where the Dalai Lama escaped. At that time, we always contacted Mr Takla Phuntsok Tashi, the husband of the Dalai Lama's elder sister, he was the chief of the security guard in Norbulingka. And so we cleared the road and reported this to him and then one night the Dalai Lama escaped. Some of our colleagues prepared the boat in yak skin to cross the river, some others were waiting for the Dalai Lama at the other side of river. I also stayed all the way with him. Fortunately we could help him to escape. So when the Chinese threw a bomb on Norbulingka, the Dalai Lama was already gone for two days.

I was fighting, then our group went to Lhoka and joined the Chushi Gangdruk. We wanted to prevent the Chinese to go to Lhasa, but it was impossible because they were everywhere. Then we escaped from Lhoka to India, we arrived in Montawang, then in Bomdila, where we received some food from the Indian government and then we moved to Misamari and built a house and stayed there more than five months. One thing was that the Indian government was so kind to us because they gave the opportunity for those under the age of twenty-five to go to school and those above this age they had to go to work. Since at that time I was around thirty, I worked in the road construction.

In 1960 I went to Mustang. In the first year we had not enough food and the accommodation was very poor. We were too many soldiers and we were also not used to this place, so some died because of the lack of food.

Text on the right side of the picture: 'Kunga, I will always pray for you'.
(*Tenzin Gyatso, 2 February 1982*)

Afterwards it was getting better and better: we got guerrilla training, we learned to read a map and a few times I went to Tibet for guerrilla but I didn't see or couldn't kill any Chinese. So I only got training in Mustang and not in the US, but some of us went there, like Tashi (interview 4) and Norbu Dorjee (interview 23), who are still living in our camp here. Bawa Yeshi went against the Tibetan policy and he split from our group.

I can tell you about my experience in Mustang and Lhasa. In Mustang, there was not much, only training for guerrilla and map reading, not that much fighting with the Chinese. In Lhasa, it was really a difficult time for us and I remember one thing that our Derge people did something very stupid: we always kept only a few bullets with us while the rest stayed in the storeroom and so one day the Chinese threw a bomb in the storeroom and at that time we were eating just nearby and many of us got injured by our own bullets, so I know we always have to be really careful and smart. After that, we hadn't much bullets left and it was even more difficult to fight the Chinese and we were so disappointed because we had been so stupid.

One thing I feel so proud of about my Derge people is that even if we had such bad facilities, we were able to help the Dalai Lama escape safely. Now I know the army always has to keep the bullets with them, since you never know where the enemy is and then you can immediately use them. That I am always remembering. So about Mustang I cannot tell you much more. I stayed there till 1971 and then they sent me to India to learn how to make Tibetan carpets and so I learned it during one year and a few months and came back to Paljorling with our carpet teacher. We started to make the carpets and we also taught some other people. First life in Paljorling was very harsh and also I got TB, that time I had lots of physical problems, but that was my karma, I couldn't do anything.

I tell you one thing about my Derge people's audience with the Dalai Lama who gave us a picture with a handwritten text and some certificate. I always kept it in a secret place and didn't show it to anybody. This is a big achievement in my life and one of the most precious things I have.

ADVICE TO THE YOUNGER GENERATION

I don't want to give any advice because young people usually don't listen! But I want to say that the most important thing is education; they have to study very hard and have to know who is the enemy and that everybody is the same, so they have to keep two different things in mind: who is the rival and who is the friend?

Interview conducted on 20 June 2007 in Paljorling.

Tashi Topgyal

I am 88 years old and my fatherland is named Lhorong, it takes seven days by foot to reach from Chamdo. My father's name was Ngodup Tsering and my mother's name was Samdon. In my family there were seven members: four brothers and one sister. I was the eldest son. We lived as a farmer and we had some yaks and cows.

Actually, Chamdo is one of the main places where the Tibetan government is represented. The Red Chinese came to Chamdo and they cheated the Tibetans telling they were going to Lhasa to help the Tibetans but they had the very bad political intention to occupy Tibet. After seven years, the fierce Mao Tse-Tung invited the Dalai Lama, who was around fifteen years old, to Beijing. After that the Chinese came to Lhasa and made an office there. Then Siling, the leader of the Chinese army camp, invited the Dalai Lama to the camp but the Tibetan people feared he would be taken to China, so thousands of Tibetans including monks, nuns and lay people surrounded the Norbulingka palace to prohibit the Dalai Lama to accept the invitation.[1] The number of Tibetan soldiers with me was between 2,000 and 3,000. In the night, the Dalai Lama escaped to India. After he left, the Chinese bombed Norbulingka and killed thousands of people including monks, nuns, and lay people. At that time I was not with the Dalai Lama, I was fighting the Chinese in Lhasa. When they heard the Dalai Lama already escaped, their anger grew and they unleashed a real war. However, the Tibetan army continued to fight with vigour; but without good weapons and proper training it was in vain. Sometimes we continued to fight, sometimes we drew back. We lost the war and gradually Tibet was wholly occupied by the Red Chinese.

In 1959, due to that, we escaped to Nepal. At that time, I was thirty-seven, Tibet was occupied by the Chinese and I sought asylum in Mustang. But first I went to India through Montawang and then to Misamari where I stayed only for one year, since the climate was too hot. Afterwards I went to Gangtok where I stayed for nearly one year and worked in the road construction, then finally I went to Mustang where I stayed for fifteen years.

REGAIN TIBET AND LIVE A FREE LIFE

The first year we had no weapons, we started to do exercises and train ourselves and stayed on the top of the hills to protect us from the Chinese soldiers. That place was empty, there was really nothing. After one year, America airdropped weapons during the night in an area in Tibet and at the same time, some Tibetans who had received training from the Americans, arrived in Mustang. We brought the weapons from Tibet to Mustang and we continued to fight the Chinese like guerrillas for fifteen years. The provision of weapons from America had encouraged us to fight the Chinese. Our main aim was to regain Tibet and to live a prosperous free life.

During that first year, we had a very difficult time, mostly we had not enough food and so sometimes at night we went to beg for food from the locals. After we got support from America, we ordered food with the locals and we also got rice from India, which was transported to Nepal by horses and mules and then through Pokhara and further up to Mustang by a shepherd, but it was still not sufficient for all of us. Our daily ration was hardly one plate of rice.

In Mustang, Bawa Yeshi was the chief leader of our camp, but he was corrupted; he appropriated nearly all the financial assistance from America for himself. We were about 2,000 soldiers, but the rumour of Bawa Yeshi's corruption divided us into two groups. Most of us didn't want to follow him, except for a few 100 who only did it for the money. He also cheated many Tibetans trained by the US to support him, but without success. After that, we didn't get time to choose another leader, because the conflict was acknowledged by the Nepalese government. When they heard about Tibetans hiding in Mustang, our organisation had to stop, since the Chinese pressured them to scatter our army camps. Bawa Yeshi secretly negotiated with the Red Chinese [in fact he negotiated with the Nepalese] to destroy our army camp in Mustang, but due to the grace of the *Kunchoksum* the plan was unsuccessful and he surrendered to the chief leader of the Nepalese government Anatadik Singh.[2] I don't know where he lived, I only know he died in Kathmandu.

So we surrendered, not because of the frightening circumstances, but rather due to the soul-stirring words of the Dalai Lama who asked us to hand in our weapons to the Nepalese government. After that, we were confined for eleven months on the hill of Nuwakot and surrounded by the Nepalese army. We were not really put in jail because there was not enough space for all of us, but we had to stay on the hill and couldn't move freely.

ADVICE TO THE YOUNGER GENERATION

Follow every word of the Dalai Lama and without discrimination between men and women, the entire Tibetan people ought to put all their efforts to free Tibet from the iron fist of the Red Chinese. I am eighty-eight now and I have been fighting since a long time and still we have to continue and hope the best, because no one knows when Tibet will be free.

Interview conducted on 8 June 2007 in Jampaling.

Lopa

During the interview he was counting the 108 beads of his mala.

I am 75 and I was born in Gawa in Kham. My father's name was Lobsang Phuntsok, whereas my mother's name was Tayak. In my family there were seven members: five boys and my parents. Our occupation was nomad.

In 1957, my village was already occupied by the Chinese. I was involved myself since my four brothers were killed by the Chinese. At that time, people from my village opposed the Chinese and only a few of us could escape, all the others were killed, especially the monks. More than 1,000 monks and lay people were killed. The Chinese also killed children because they planned to raze the village. At twenty-five, I escaped to Lhasa and stayed there for one year.

In 1959, I joined the Chushi Gangdruk and they sent me to Norbulingka to be a secret guard for the Dalai Lama. There were four different gates, I stayed at the east gate.

More than 1,000 people surrounded Norbulingka to protect the Dalai Lama. In the early morning, the Chinese bombed Norbulingka and at that time, I saw dead bodies everywhere and of course we couldn't oppose the Chinese because we had no good weapons, so that's why I ran away from there to Lhoka without shoes. With a group we escaped to India, to Montawang.

In 1959, I was already in India in Darjeeling; I worked on the road for one year. Then, the Tibetan government restarted the Chushi Gangdruk, so I joined in 1960 and went to Mustang. First, our condition was very poor. We had not enough food and we slept under the trees. The climate was very cold and I had one blanket, which I had to share.

CHINESE DOCUMENTS

In the beginning, we started the training with a stick; after that we got weapons from the US and we were more confident to fight the Chinese. A few times I went with a group to Tibet to fight the Chinese; we fought for one or two hours and then we drew back, we were always doing a guerrilla fight.

Once, our group destroyed a Chinese truck, that time we got these important documents from China. I don't know exactly how important they were, but we sent them later to Dharamsala and now the Tibetan government is keeping them. [In fact they were sent to the CIA]

In 1972, we came to Pokhara, we started to build the Annapurna hotel; at that time we had such a big land, but the Nepalese took it from us and didn't pay us. While I stayed in the Tibetan settlement, my life was like a normal life and we got lots of support from the Tibetan government.

ADVICE TO THE YOUNGER GENERATION

Usually the young generation doesn't listen to the older one. So if I tell them our story, they feel bored to listen. That is a very bad habit in our camp.

Important things to remember are to keep the Tibetan culture and religion alive. We have such an important culture, that's very useful for our life in exile and the new generation has to know this. Like a monk who has to know how to teach about peace, I, as a nomad, I know how to take care of the animals, how to survive with them. All this, when we get our freedom, the younger generation should know. Because in exile already two generations passed, so the third generation has to know this and take their responsibility for the country.

Interview conducted on 19 June 2007 in Paljorling.

Tashi Tsering

During the interview he was very serious; he felt it was very important to tell his story. Kunga (interview 27) intervened 'for support'. Sometimes they were arguing about who was going to speak first.

I am 75 years old and I was born in Gyalthang in Kham. My father's name was Pema Wangchuk, whereas my mother's was Tashi Dolma. In my family we were nine members, including mother and father, five sons and two daughters. I don't know what happened with my family in Tibet, it's very difficult to contact them. When I was in Tibet, I was a businessman, I was selling horses and donkeys.

I joined the Chushi Gangdruk in 1957. At that time, they organised to make a golden throne for the Dalai Lama, the leader was Andrug Gompo Tashi. I was in Lhasa then, but in 1958 I moved to Lhoka where the whole Tibetan army was. In 1959 the Chinese invited the Dalai Lama to take him to China, so we all Tibetans were worried, especially the Chushi Gangdruk. So we protected him, thousands of people surrounded Norbulingka; one night the Dalai Lama left from there to Lhoka. We who lived in Lhoka were fully responsible to wait for him at the other side of the river. Then we stayed in Lhoka and the Dalai Lama quickly left to Montawang.

Our group was fighting the Chinese and it was impossible because there were so many, we killed hundreds and hundreds of them, still there were getting more and more. Then we also escaped to Montawang and during our journey we killed many Chinese and also they killed lots of our soldiers and common people. At that time we were 1,000 of people: women, men and children, not only soldiers, and we also had to protect them. It was very difficult when the Chinese threw a bomb and killed many people. When we arrived in Magola, there was a high mountain topped with snow, the Chinese followed us, they again threw a very heavy bomb, but it was incredible, nobody died and nothing happened. Then we crossed the mountain and arrived in Montawang. The Indians sent us to Misamari, they gave us a job in the road construction in Gangtok. I worked there for seven or eight months, the living conditions were very bad but we had no other choice.

All the Tibetans asked the leaders to organise something for the army or against China and they started to collect people and sent them to Mustang. I arrived there in September 1960. It's probably the same as all the others already told you: in the beginning it was very hard, especially the lack of food, and also we didn't know the area, we came from a very hot place and we didn't have enough clothes while Mustang was a very cold place.

AIR-DROPPED WEAPONS

In Lektse Tsongra in Tibet, we fought the Chinese in a guerrilla fight; we didn't know how many Chinese there were or how many of them we have killed. I didn't get any training from the Americans, but those who got a training came to Mustang and taught us map reading, fighting and guerrilla techniques.

I saw the US supported us, one time airplanes were coming to Mustang, but the weather was very bad and there was such a strong wind, so they couldn't throw all the weapons. Finally they did on the Tibetan side of the border. I went there to pick them up and took them back to Mustang. I heard a story about this airplane, but I am not sure if it's true or not. Since for this airplane it was very difficult to drop the weapons, they missed the place and flew into Tibet from west to east in Chamdo. This is what I heard.

I know Bawa Yeshi but we were not close, he was our first leader in Mustang; then Gen Wangdu became our leader and Lhamo Tsering, the secretary. So some people said there were some problems between them, but I honestly don't know what happened. Later Bawa Yeshi formed another group and then took the money from the army salary, but I don't know how much he took. Anyway, he already died.

SUCCESSFUL RAID

During my experience in Mustang, sometimes I went to Tibet as a guerrilla to kill some Chinese and put a bomb on the road. Once we collected some information to send to the US. One day we attacked one truck and there were some soldiers and we killed them all and there were also documents. I was with this group, but I was not involved; I was at a distance. We got so many documents and weapons and we took pictures of all the documents and gave it to the US and they were very happy and told us this was a wonderful job and they thanked us for this success.

I stayed in Mustang for fourteen years, from 1960 till 1974. Finally, the Chinese put lots of pressure on the Nepalese government, this government is so poor, they had no power at that time, they told us our army camp had to be closed and we had to give all the weapons to them and they promised us that in exchange of all the weapons, they would give us a settlement. But it was our wish to live in Mustang, we lived there since fourteen years and we knew how to arrange our live; so at that time we had lots of problems with the Nepalese government. Most of the Tibetans didn't want to surrender because our way of thinking was that our motherland was already occupied by the Chinese and the Nepalese didn't want us to live here, so then we really had nothing. So we wanted to fight them and most of us were already prepared, but then the message of the Dalai Lama came with the information to surrender to the Nepalese and to live in peace with them and to use no violence. If we fought with them, still we wouldn't have any country. Then we felt so sad and many of us cried and some of us committed suicide, because when we gave the weapons back, we had nothing left. So our leader Gen Wangdu advised us: "Don't kill yourself, there is no reason, we will never give up".

So we gave all the weapons to the Nepalese. Then they immediately changed [their plans]: we were not allowed to stay in Mustang, we had to go down and they put us in jail in Nuwakot for five or six months. But, they didn't use violence, we were free to go out. After our release, we moved to Kotre Kohla, then to Jampaling.

Later, we built a carpet factory in Paljorling and I worked there. In the beginning I didn't know how to do. It was very difficult to study but the work was easy because you could look how other people did the work, how they moved. First we had to wash the wool, then we made carpets. In my life the only thing I know is how to make a carpet.

In 1997, our business went down and the carpet factory was closed.

ADVICE TO THE YOUNGER GENERATION

I want to tell you my own experience, so that is my kind of advice for the young Tibetans. We are the first generation and it comes almost to an end, like the second generation; but the third generation they have to learn many things. So my generation, if we want to go back, the Chinese will not accept and if we want to fight them, we have not enough energy. The second generation, most of them were born in very bad conditions, so they don't know that much; but the third generation they are very lucky, they were born in the best conditions, whatever they want to study they get the chance to and also to see the whole world. But those young people, most of them, they don't want to listen to the stories of our Tibetan lives.

We have to think carefully about the Dalai Lama, if he is not alive anymore, then Tibet will come to an end because since 1959 till now only he was fighting the Chinese and travelling all over the world to ask for help to support Tibet. If he dies, who will support us?

That's why the young people have to be very careful. I can tell you my life, I left Mustang when I was forty-six years old and I got married when I was forty-eight, so when my first son was born, I was fifty; with my first daughter I was fifty-four, so when I want to help them, I have not much energy since I am already old. And by the time they will be old enough to look after their parents, we will already have passed away.

The young generation has to think about the Nepalese situation: the Nepalese government is not always reliable, so one day we might get so much suffering again, even people of my age. I am always worrying about this. That's why the youngsters have to learn Tibetan, have to study very hard and take care of our future.

Interview conducted on 20 June 2007 in Paljorling.

Chime Phuntsok

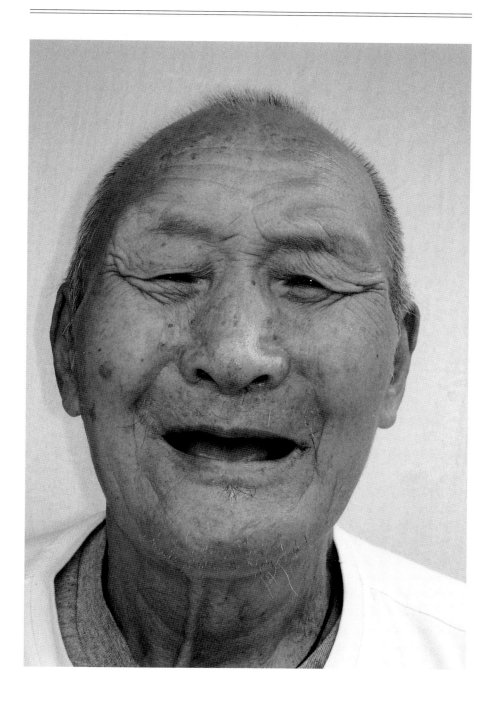

It was not possible to interview this man, since he had become almost deaf and mentally weak. However he possessed a thirty-five-page booklet called *A Real Life-History of Freedom fighter Mod-kham Drayab-pa Chime Phuntsok*. I was told the author was someone from Dharamsala. You can find some excerpts below.

I am 83 years old and I was born in Drayab in Kham. My father's name was Nyocho Ma-Gon Nye-Gu Drong-Medh-Tsang and my mother's name Donlha. My occupation was monk. In 1938, I became monk in the Ganden monastery while I was on pilgrimage in Lhasa.

In 1958, 217 monks of this monastery were recruited in the Chushi Gangdruk; we left our monastery at night. The group was divided into three groups and I took the responsibility of 100 people and set out to Tsetang (Lhoka).

On 9 March 1959, it became clear that the Dalai Lama would arrive the next day and I left together with thirteen other fighters for Dranang where we arrived at 10 a.m. As soon as we arrived, we received the blessing of His Holiness. There were around 200 people with him, including high officials, guards and family members. As he would be visiting Jampaling [he speaks about a monastery in Tibet, not about the camp where he is living now], the residents were waiting for his blessing with incense and white painted stones lined on both sides of the path.

ON THE WAY WITH THE DALAI LAMA

Later, Phala gave the order that we had to go to Za-Pho pass and the Chushi Gangdruk force accompanied His Holiness. While crossing the pass, we had a small rest on the top and two pictures were taken: one on which we were all standing, was taken by His Holiness and one with His Holiness sitting in the middle was taken by Phuntsok Tashi.[1] We all arrived safely in the Chongye Chenye monastery. Phala interrogated me about our battles against the Chinese in Tsetang. He said that at any cost we could not let go Tsetang in the hands of the Chinese, since it would be an obstacle for His Holiness' escape in exile. He assured to provide us the necessary ammunitions and forces and indeed 100 Chugang [Chushi Gangdruk] forces with heavy arms came to receive us.

We then left with mixed feelings: our success in bringing His Holiness in exile gave us an immense feeling of joy, but it saddened us a lot to be departed from him. In Tsetang we fought many times against the Chinese till His Holiness reached Montawang. At last we had to leave the spot since we ran out of bullets. [...]

Then, we set out to Tsona to meet the Chugang force, but our fighters were already defeated leaving eight badly injured persons behind. While on our way, Chinese airplanes flew over us but couldn't see us and so we were not hurt.

FOOD BY AIR

Then finally we reached Montawang in Indian territory. As soon as we reached there, we surrendered ourselves to the Indian government. We handed over our arms and in turn they issued us the receipts. We were provided food by air, thrice a day. We could use the empty bags for our own purposes, so we used them as clothes and mattress and remained there for fifteen days waiting for Aadruk Jundak, one of our chiefs. After his arrival, we were sent to Misamari in groups of fifty persons a day. It took us four days to reach there. On our way we were provided food and shelter. In Misamari, the Indian government gave us food, shelter, clothes, medicines, etc. and we stayed there for about three months.

As it became very hot, we were allowed to leave for Sikkim to work in the road construction. I worked in Drejong [= Denjong, Tibetan for Sikkim] as a day labour for about one year, bearing lots of hardships. We were paid two Rupees a day as a wage.

A HARSH WINTER IN MUSTANG

Aadruk Jundak informed us about the newly established Mustang base and I, along with other friends from Drayab and Chatreng, left for Darjeeling. We received 160 Rupees as travel expenditure and we were provided maps, so that we could travel by foot. It took us twenty-five days to reach Yarabug.

Bawa Yeshi, the chief leader, divided us into eight battalions. For about three months, we received American guerrilla training using false wooden guns. We had a ration of three shells of maize flour a day, due to scarcity of food we were forced to consume leather goods. We spent one winter in the pine wood without proper clothes and shelter.

In March 1961, nine people along with arms for 800 people were dropped by the CIA in Tibet. We went to collect the arms. Four battalions were formed with fifty fighters from each of the eight battalions and we were dispatched to Tibet. I was trained by Chatreng Kowa Tenpa who followed a six-month guerrilla training in the US. In the summer of 1961, with ten people and horses lend by the nomads, we prepared ourselves for the first confrontation with twenty Chinese and we were able to kill fourteen of them. After twenty-five minutes of firing, the standard in guerrilla fighting, we withdrew and returned to our base and reached there after two days. In the winter of 1961 a new arms drop occurred; the temperature was so low that some of us suffered from frostbite while carrying the weapons to the base.

MORE FIGHTING

During the summer of 1962, we were ordered to go with twenty-five horsemen to Mugu Bazaar, where Nepalese and Chinese traders met. I was responsible for the expenses and received one coin for food for each of them. We were all courageous and well-armed. Just before reaching Mugu, we spotted fifty Chinese soldiers with 1,000 sheep and goats loaded with food. While fifteen of us attacked the soldiers, the remaining ten drove the flocks. Four of their soldiers were killed and three rifles confiscated, we didn't loose anybody. Returning back, we were highly appreciated by Bawa Yeshi and given fifty Rupees and a full-day party.

[...]

   In 1965, we had to look for a new place to establish a base for 100 fighters; we found Pema Tsal. I was sent with two other men to Kathmandu to work as secret agents. Under the cover of businessmen, we opened a restaurant to be able to supply food to the new base. Not to arouse the villagers' suspicion that so much food was sent to an inhabited place, we told them a high Lama would come there and many old people would attend his preaching and that all the food was prepared for them. The Nepalese government was informed about the rumour of arms and came to Pema Tsal to check, but the weapons had been hidden together with most of the food supplies.

SURRENDER & ARRESTS

In 1974, 2,000 Nepali soldiers reached Mustang and asked us to surrender peacefully; if not, they would force us to get out of the region. Gadon Wangdu announced that he would not surrender at any cost but would rather affront them. But then in this emergency situation, Takla Phuntsok Tashi from the Tibetan government in India arrived with the taped message of H. H. in which he asked us to surrender. So we did and handed over the weapons to the Nepalese government and were driven out of Mustang to Pokhara. Seven important persons were arrested including Lhamo Tsering, while Gadon Wangdu was killed on his way while fleeing to India. Thus our Mustang force disintegrated and came to an end. [...]

I had the opportunity to have a private meeting with H. H. for about half an hour. He said to me: "You have done well till now and you shouldn't be sad about the end of the Mustang force. I have sent twice a petition to his Majesty the King of Nepal but didn't get any reply. Being a refugee, there is no effect. Anyway it doesn't matter. Go to Pokhara and don't be sad". So he patted me and touched my forehead with his forehead.

ADVICE TO THE YOUNGER GENERATION

The big loss caused by our enemy, the Red Chinese, must never be forgotten by the young Tibetans and I request to every tsampa eating Tibetan to work according to H. H. the Dalai Lama's ideology and to be able to face the difficulties on the way while struggling for the cause of Independence.

He is still living in Jampaling.

Dorjee Wangdu

He passed away on 8 January 2009 in Varanasi (India) while attending a teaching of the Dalai Lama.

I am 65 years old [he is confused about his age] and I was told that I was born in Lhasa. My father's name was Tsewang Gyaltsen, whereas I don't remember my mother's because I was very small when she died. I had one sister and we were nomads. In Tarong* near Lekshe it was peaceful and I was a nomad and was busy with cattle, sheep and yaks till I came to Mustang.

When I was in Tibet, I heard about a Chushi Gangdruk army cantonment in Tarong. I have seen three or four Chinese, they came to our area, they worked there and they didn't interfere in my work or didn't do atrocities to us. They were speaking very politely and they offered us eatable things, sweets and tsampa.

I came out of Tibet along with my father on a pilgrimage to Nepal and he left me with a Lama in a monastery in Sagarbug in Mustang, telling me he would come back, but he never returned. I knew he died at the age of more than forty. He went back to Tarong to look after the animals, we had 10 yaks and 100 sheep and goats.

My brother-in-law asked me to join the army in India. In 1959, I went to Delhi and when I reached there, it was not to join the army but to work as a gatekeeper. Later, I became a cook.

INSTEAD OF SITTING IDLE

I heard about the Dalai Lama's flight when I was there and I felt that our country was lost and that it was my duty to do something for my government, so I joined in 1964 at the age of fifteen. During that time, there were some instructions that all should do so and we were forcibly made to join. An order came that instead of sitting idle you had to join. I haven't fought the Chinese face to face but I went to Sangdak to patrol the area and see if there were any Chinese. I stayed there for around three years.

I was not in training in the US, that time ten group leaders and teachers were sent to the US.

I remember that in Mustang I used to go out in the camp with a gun on my shoulder, and there were very nice weapons that I could rely on more than on my companions.

I only came to know about Bawa Yeshi later on. In the beginning he was a good leader, but there were problems among the leaders and all the money was used by themselves. Bawa Yeshi has given some money to the Nepalese officials and he left no money for the common soldiers, that is why he got the Nepalese citizenship.

I stayed in Mustang till 1974. Afterwards, I was in Nuwakot jail and then I was sent to Kotre Kohla and afterwards I shifted to Jampaling settlement.

I went to 'Tenshug' in Dharamsala and I met the Dalai Lama. He asked me: "Where are you from?" I replied that I was from Drayab [Lhasa?] and I received his blessing, some pills and a scarf. I will pray for his long life and that Tibet will get freedom soon.

ADVICE TO THE YOUNGER GENERATION

My advice is to do your study hard and that children should go to school regularly and reach the highest possible degree. Two of my children are also going to school, one is in grade X and one is in grade VII. You should also be more responsible for your country.

Interview conducted on 23 June 2007 in Jampaling.

Phuntsok

While telling his story, he lectured the young interviewer who sometimes interrupted him.

I am 61 years old and I was born in U-Tsang in a place called Dongpa. Both my father Tsewang and my mother Palzom passed away long time ago. My family consisted of nine members, I had three brothers and three sisters. Unfortunately, my eldest brother was killed by the Chinese army during the occupation. During that time, Dongpa was known to be an area specifically meant for salt mining. People used to take lots of salt from there. Agriculture and nomad were the primary sources of livelihood for my parents. They used yaks and sheep as means of transportation for the salt; sheep and goats could carry four bags and yaks nine or ten. We had altogether between 500 and 3,000 sheep next to 200 yaks and 8 or 9 horses.

SUICIDE

In 1963, I escaped from Tibet and left my parents and family behind. From then till 1967, I was begging in the street and had no job. Then I came to know about the Chushi Gangdruk in Mustang, I was single and young and I got enrolled at the age of twenty-one or twenty-two; only unmarried men were allowed at that time. My motivation was that I knew Tibet's condition and I wanted to fight the Chinese and regain our independence. We should have our own culture and identity which should be protected. For this purpose, I got military training and it was a new experience rather than staying redundant.

After 1959, my parents were put in prison and other people were arrested too, so people became terrified of speaking frankly. I have also seen many people who were scared to be tortured and committed suicide by jumping into the river instead. That is a bad memory I have.

You may have inquired our senior people and leaders, they might have given you lots of information about Bawa Yeshi, so I think I cannot add anything. He was known as the general leader and in Mustang he was the sole responsible for administrating the Lo-Drik-Tsug during the most difficult period with lack of food and transportation. He has done a good job, but after 1970 we, the common people, had no big problem with him, but the leaders had. They had their own ideas and this created a clash between them. Now most of the Lo-Drik-Tsug are living in Jampaling and Paljorling, although there is a vast number of them scattered everywhere in India, especially in Dharamsala. The Lo-Drik-Tsug is not an organisation from one region in Tibet, but from all three regions and that's why they have been dispersed. The people who were against Bawa Yeshi are now mostly in Jampaling and Paljorling.

My life in Paljorling was not so difficult compared with my escape from Tibet. I started to work as a carpet weaver and the houses and infrastructure were also good at that time. Now the carpet business is very low and lots of us are jobless, not only from our settlements, but in whole Nepal each person involved in this carpet business faces the same problem.

ADVICE TO THE YOUNGER GENERATION

From the point of view of education, I have nothing to say to the youngsters because I have never seen a school, not for a single day. But from my experience I want to say that every youngster should be very sincere and live honestly and be very cordial and friendly with local people as well as neighbours, they should look after their old parents and take care of the old people.

Interview conducted on 19 June 2007 in Paljorling.

Sangye Gonpo

Sometimes, he had to dig deeply in his memory to remember a place name, but he was very expressive in his speech, using his small umbrella as a gun or laughing out, telling they had to run from the Chinese, or giving his advice for the youngsters.

I am 73 and I was born in Kanze which is in Kham. The area was named Thame [= corner] Gyaltaktsang [= a family name]. My father's name was

Yonten and my mother's name was Pema Choedon. In my family we were four brothers and one sister. Mother died when I was around seven years old. I was the second youngest. Our occupation in Tibet was agriculture.

In 1956, when I was twenty-three, I wanted to join the Chushi Gangdruk. That time in the south-east the situation was deteriorating, there were lots of Chinese army troops who destroyed all the holy places and caught the leaders of the monasteries and the rich people. And so then we decided to go to Lhasa by horse, we were about sixty people. When I reached Phenpo at midnight I tried to join the Chushi Gangdruk and we left from there to Tsurphu. The Chinese were shooting at us and they hit our group. I was injured and couldn't move anymore, so I stayed with my family for about one month. Then I went to Lhasa to meet my brother who invited a Tibetan doctor; after one month I was healthy again and I stayed with my brother till Losar [Tibetan New Year].

NORBULINGKA'S 'SIEGE'

After Losar, I went to the Jokhang temple [main temple in Lhasa] for praying and in March the problem around Norbulingka started. I was sitting on the backside of a friend's bicycle, but it was impossible to get inside; there was a huge crowd of men and women in front of Norbulingka. I was also attending there because the Chinese had invited the Dalai Lama in their army camp, so people from all over Tibet were very angry and they blocked all the entrances of Norbulingka. In the early morning, we heard the sound of guns and later the Chinese threw a bomb outside Norbulingka, but we didn't see any of them. Then they threw a bomb inside Norbulingka and continued to shoot and they killed lots of people. All the area was covered with dead bodies. So I think they already planned this right from the beginning. Most of us ran away from there, but I was thinking why are they running away since the Dalai Lama is still inside. So I decided not to run but to stay to protect him and the Tibetan people. Me and two friends entered the summer palace. In the outside boundary on the top of the gate was a check post with some weapons and we started shooting at the Chinese from there.

Later, we thought that since all the people were running away, maybe the Dalai Lama was not there anymore, so we decided to run away too. The Chinese threw a bomb, so I had difficulties to run and follow my friend due to my leg problem. So I just hid there until dark and went back in the direction of Norbulingka. There it was difficult to walk, because it was so muddy. Then we continued to the Drepung hill, where some families welcomed us and gave us tsampa and tea. And still we heard the sound of bombs and guns coming from Norbulingka's side. We carried on to the area of *Drepung* Loseling monastery, Phenpo and again we were welcomed by the storeroom-keeper with tsampa and eatable things and we were also given a horse to ride.

CHINESE ATTACKS

At that time, we were fourteen people. We planned to join the Chushi Gangdruk, so we went to Phoedo. On the way, the Chinese were shooting, the army was everywhere, even airplanes were surrounding us from the sky. We met several horse riding people and told them we also wanted to join the Chushi Gangdruk but they explained us that since the Chushi Gangdruk was destroyed, it was impossible to go and they had chosen another direction. So, we followed them.

One old man from the other group told us that since there was no way to join the Chushi Gangdruk, no way to fight the Chinese, it would be better to go to the Mt Kailash area [in Tibetan Ghang Rinpoche, sacred mountain], because maybe there were no Chinese and we could make a new plan. So we were near the Kongpo area and headed in the direction of Mt Kailash. On the way we kept on fighting and had lots of problems. Some day we relaxed and when we reached the area of Yagjetanga*, our horses couldn't move anymore since their feet were too painful, so we freed them to relax. After some days, we saw somebody coming pretty far away from us, then we watched very carefully and they were Chinese coming to us. Immediately we packed everything and caught our horse, but before we finished packing the Chinese already started shooting. The horses ran away and I couldn't catch my horse, but luckily I caught the horse of one of my colleagues. One of our group members was killed and we left in a hurry.

From our group, only three people were lucky to still have their horse. We continued our trip to Mt Kailash but we didn't reach there. We reached Zonga, and later on we reached the Kyirong area to enter the Nepal boundary. We handed over all our weapons to the Nepalese army and they seemed very happy and they told us: "Dalai Lama India, Dalai Lama India". We didn't understand anything, but now I think they told us the Dalai Lama was already in India and we were also sent there.

So we reached Kathmandu with our horses and we stayed with Gyal Lama and we sold all our horses to him; each horse for 400 coins. At that time, there were only coins, no notes. It was big money; we received a good price, I think it is like 200 Rupees now. We stayed in Kathmandu, there is a Mongolian monastery.[1] We visited it several times to pray and also other holy places in Kathmandu.

Then we departed for India, Kalimpong. It was amazing because even though we didn't speak a word of the language, we always arrived where we wanted. During this stay we had some eatable things, but it was not enough for our stomach. We stayed there for one month; at that time we had the option to study or to work.

One of the leaders told me: "You are young, you are twenty-five, for you it is better to go to school in Misamari, Darjeeling or Kalimpong". But, I heard about the people working in the road construction in Gangtok, and I wanted to join there for some months. Then the Chushi Gangdruk started collecting people to fight again the Chinese, and so I went to Mustang in 1960 and stayed there till 1974.

SHOPKEEPER

During our stay in Mustang, I didn't have that much experience, but we had guerrilla war training, we learned to handle weapons, and other necessary things like to read a map. In the beginning, it was a very difficult time to get to know this place and also we had not enough food; we were hungry almost every day. After some years, I was responsible to pay the wages, a sort of accountant. That time we formed one big group divided in fifteen groups under Bawa Yeshi's responsibility. After some years, I became shopkeeper of the resistance. During that time as a shopkeeper, one day Bawa Yeshi went down to Pokhara and some people rushed with him, but I stayed in Mustang. We didn't know exactly what was the problem.

In 1974, the Nepalese army came to Mustang to get our weapons but we were not happy to give them back. After some days, the Dalai Lama's representative arrived and brought the Dalai Lama's message; we listened and handed over our weapons to the Nepalese government. Then we went down to the area of Nuwakot and stayed there a couple of months. A few months later, we shifted to Kotre Kohla and to Tashi Ling, then to Jampaling settlement. Since we lived there, life was much better and we were free to do what we wanted. Between 1974 till 1980, I stayed outside this camp in a Nepali village, it was not that much difficult because there were so many Tibetans around. In 1980 I joined this camp to work as a cashier till 1990.

ADVICE TO THE YOUNGER GENERATION

I don't have any education, so I don't know how to give any advice, but I will tell what I saw in my life, so the younger generation has to take this good chance to study and always follow the best advice of the Dalai Lama and the Tibetan government. Never forget we are refugees living in exile. So you have to be simple and honest and keep our Tibetan identity.

Interview conducted on 19 June 2007 in Paljorling.

Samphel

I am 75 years old and I was born in Drakyab Magon in Kham. My father's name was Dodak, whereas my mother's name was Zomkyi. In our family we were four members: one sister, me and my parents; and I was a monk in Ganden monastery.

BODYGUARD

In 1958, I joined the Chushi Gangdruk at the age of twenty-five in Drikuthang in the Lhoka district. When the Chinese occupied Tibet and Lhasa, I was together with the Dalai Lama from Lhasa to Lhoka and till the border. I was like a bodyguard, we were eighty people. Of course it was really difficult to pay attention and not to worry. When we safely reached the border, we felt relieved but still I cannot understand my feelings: from one side I was happy that he was safe, but on the other hand our country was already in Chinese hands. Afterwards we went back to Lhoka to continue the fighting. I don't remember if I have killed Chinese on the way, but I do remember that we were always shooting. The Chinese threw bombs and were shooting on us, but nobody was killed at that time thanks to the protective amulet [gawu] from the Dalai Lama. We couldn't really challenge the Chinese because we were outnumbered by them.

Afterwards we reached Magola and then India. I was not in training in US, but I was in Misamari at that time. From there we went to Sikkim for the road construction.

A HARD TIME

In 1960, me and our group reached Mustang and joined the Lo-Drik-Tsug organisation. There we suffered a lot, we ate boiled yak skin. Of course we were soldiers, so we had to do physical exercises, but we had not much energy so it was very hard. It is difficult to explain in words what a difficult situation we faced there. Afterwards, we got support from the Americans, so we had no financial problems and good army facilities. Then we could go to the border to fight the Chinese and we fought them very successfully.

Bawa Yeshi was first the leader of the Lo-Drik-Tsug and after some years there was a problem between the leaders. I don't know exactly what was the real problem. Then Bawa Yeshi did corruption of the army finances and he acted against Tibetans. So he was like part of the Chinese. I stayed in Mustang for fourteen years. During that time, I always wanted to fight the Chinese and get my country back. Unfortunately we didn't get the chance and later the Nepalese government made problems and first we really wanted to fight them; but then we got the message from the Dalai Lama and the Tibetan government that told us to hand over our weapons to them. So we surrendered, then the Nepalese government put us in the Nuwakot jail and told us to join Bawa Yeshi's group, but we didn't.

Afterwards, we were sent to Pokhara and we started a Tibetan colony and lived in Jampaling settlement, I have been living here for more than thirty

The Dalai Lama and his entourage passing through a village while escaping.
(*TibetMuseum/DIIR*)

years. But, I am always remembering and wishing Tibetans will get freedom from China soon, because I want to leave my body in Tibet. Now I have lots of problems: I have a knee problem, my wife a leg problem and one of my daughters a mental one. I am always worried who will take care of her after my death.

I went for 'Tenshug' to Dharamsala and I was happy to meet my old colleagues. I remember the Dalai Lama asked me if I had got any trouble on the way back and he told me before leaving that we would meet soon one day. He also told us that we were seeking for autonomy now, not for independence. And that this was not good only for him, but for all the Tibetans; so all together we had to do the effort to attain this, it would be much better.

ADVICE TO THE YOUNGER GENERATION

All the Tibetans have to work for the Tibetan autonomy, keep the Tibetan culture alive and respect the Dalai Lama.

Interview conducted on 23 June 2007 in Jampaling.

Jampa Norbu

I am 80 years old and I was born in Tsawa Dzogang in Kham. My father's name was Tsering Tenzin, whereas my mother's name was Bhumo Yeshi. We were seven members in our family: three boys and two sisters and my parents. Our occupation was farmer.

I didn't see any atrocities of the Chinese before I joined the Chushi Gangdruk. At that time I was twenty-nine. Andrug Gompo Tashi had declared that they wanted to establish some security bodyguard for the Dalai Lama and conduct 'Tenshug' for him as he was too young. I got the order from him to be a security guard; so I did. When I joined in 1959, I left my parents and everything behind and had only guns with me. On the way some friends and three brothers were with me. I saw the Chinese kill my three brothers and one friend, but I couldn't do anything. Later, I reached Drikuthang where almost 1,000 soldiers were also killed by them.

'TENSHUG' FOR PROTECTION

The Chushi Gangdruk organised a Buddhist ceremony and a 'Tenshug', because Gompo Tashi was thinking the Dalai Lama was too young and if something happened to him, we had to pray for his long life. They asked the Dalai Lama which place was the best for the establishment of the Chushi Gangdruk: east, west, south or north. That time he told us to go to the north part of Tibet, to a place named Drikuthang. That is why I was not in Lhasa when the Chinese invited him to Silingpu [the Chinese army camp in Lhasa]. The people from Lhasa worried and didn't want him to go. More and more people surrounded Norbulingka and nobody could go in or out. One night, following the plan of some Chushi Gangdruk members, the Dalai Lama escaped quietly together with some soldiers. On the way they climbed a hill, while on the top there were lots of Chinese soldiers. But, the Dalai Lama and the Tibetan soldiers crossed in the middle of the hill and nobody saw or shot them. I believe he was protected by 'Lha Choekyong Sungma'.[1] I was with him after he just left Norbulingka. We helped him to cross the river but we stayed only for one night and one day on the other side of the river to stop the Chinese. Then he stayed in the Mendorling monastery for a few days and left from there to the border, leaving some precious pills for the soldiers with a message: "Eat three pills each day and you will not be hungry or tired or get any other problem".

INDIAN HOSPITALITY

When the Dalai Lama escaped to Montawang, we also reached there but we were more than fifty and unable to enter India. When he arrived, he first met Jawaharlal Nehru [Indian Prime Minister at that time] asking refuge for him and all the Tibetans and requesting they would not be deported to Tibet and handed over to the Chinese government. Nehru promised him all Tibetans could stay in India. At that time, the American government also invited the Dalai Lama, but Nehru requested him to stay in India telling he would take care of them.

In the meantime we fought against the Chinese. For five Chinese soldiers, our leader sent ten Tibetan soldiers to fight, but later the Chinese soldiers increased in number. Due to that, Andrug Gompo Tashi gave the order to flee to India. So, we fled one month later than the Dalai Lama. I stayed in Misamari in India for five or six months. Then we were sent to Gangtok for the road construction. We stayed there for one year. Then we travelled to Darjeeling where we stayed for three months. Afterwards, we reached Raxaul at the Nepalese border; we were stopped there for four months.

DISUNITY AMONG US

We fled to Kathmandu and then to Manang, from Manang we went to Chumi Gyatsa [Muktinath]. Then at last, we reached Yarabug where Lo-Drik-Tsug soldiers lived. That time we had lots of food problems. We ate boiled leather and suffered sometimes from hunger. Later we got support from the American government and our situation improved a lot.

[Do you know some soldiers who went for training to the US?]

I know the teacher named Lobsang Jampa but he died and I know Norbu Dorjee [interview 23]. The first time the Americans threw weapons from the airplane I was not there, but the second time I was. In Mustang, before we got American support, our livelihood was very poor. Every soldier had no good clothes to wear and also our health was too poor due to the insufficient food. Later, when we got support from the Americans our living conditions ameliorated.

Bawa Yeshi did corruption and he didn't want to give us the army salary in time. I didn't go for training to the US. That time I only had to take care of the weapons and couldn't fight the Chinese. I had to distribute the weapons to the different groups.

I stayed in Mustang for fifteen years. I have no more experience as I looked after the weapons. Later when there occurred a conflict between Bawa Yeshi and Gadon Wangdu, I was a security guard of Gadon Wangdu. So when later a battle took place between them, I was there. Then Bawa Yeshi left Yarabug and he set off to Shimbug and from there to Jomsom. Bawa Yeshi had a picnic for three days. Knowing these facts, our groups went to fight him. Later he fled to the Annapurna [hotel in Pokhara] where he had a picnic for seven days. He then fled to Manang, because his groups had stayed there. We got the order from our leaders to fight him. So we, thirty soldiers went to fight him in Manang. In our group five soldiers were spying, five were cook and five were load carrier, fifteen soldiers were carrying machine guns with each twenty bullets. I was one who carried machine guns. To reach to Bawa Yeshi's place we first had to cross a bridge. But at that time, it was damaged, so we planned to cut a big tree and put it on the bridge. There wasn't any hand-hold, so one of our soldiers fell down from the bridge and was washed away by the river. Actually the river was too deep and it was hard to find the dead body. The rest of our soldiers were able to cross the bridge. After crossing it we found a big fort built by them in the middle of the hill. We approached, but no one was living there. Then we went to the Khado river where Bawa Yeshi's group had a party for three days. On the way we killed three or four of his soldiers. That time there were 100 soldiers of him and we were twenty, so if they weren't having this party, we would have been killed. When Bawa Yeshi's group started to battle, me and some soldier friends, were in the middle part of the hill. That time I only brought machine guns and my friends brought ordinary guns. One of my friends was killed by Bawa Yeshi's group. So he fell down the cliff and we couldn't find the dead body.

SURRENDER

I lived in Mustang till 1974. Later, we were asked to give our weapons to the Nepalese government. We didn't give them back until we heard the Dalai Lama's recorded message. Along with his security bodyguard named Mr Dapon, we got this message in Kag.[2] The message said: "This time you should give your weapons to the Nepalese government. If you continue to fight a battle then your aim of getting independence will be blocked. If you give them back right now and later a battle will take place, I will be responsible for the weapons." Some of the leaders were saying not to hand over their weapons to the Nepalese government, but I, as the weapons stock keeper, I told them I wanted to hand them all over and so I did; and later all the leaders and soldiers did the same. Then we were sent to the Nuwakot jail, from there to Kotre Khola and finally we reached Jampaling.

[Was it difficult to adapt in this environment? Was it hard to start a new life here?]

Due to the Dalai Lama's gratitude, I have nothing to say. Here I live very happily and peacefully. Now I have reached the age of eighty, I have no parents. Till now I remain happily by praying to the Dalai Lama, he is great.

ADVICE TO THE YOUNGER GENERATION

You, the youngsters have to obey the elders and obey the Dalai Lama's advice and follow it. When you are going to elect people, be more just. Don't vote for your devotees, because only a just man can rule the country properly.

Interview conducted on 1 July 2007 in Jampaling.

Jampa Choedak

I am 80 years old and I was born in Jhang Nanning in U-Tsang. My father's name was Tamdin Tsering, whereas my mother's name was Kelsang. In fact, I had two mothers and one father and they had lots of children, twelve in total. Each mother got five sons and one daughter. Our occupation was farmer and I was a monk.

DRAGGED BY A DONKEY

When the Chinese invaded Eastern Tibet around 1940, [1950] the Tibetan representative's office was in Chamdo. Some soldiers were also there and my elder brother joined them voluntarily. Later, the Chinese started to occupy the whole of Tibet, so then the Chushi Gangdruk began around 1957 and later I also joined them.

In 1959, I was still a monk in the Gaden Choekhor monastery and the Chushi Gangdruk came there to ask for weapons. Later, I heard about the Chinese atrocities but I haven't seen them myself. They destroyed my monastery and killed lots of village people and monks. Especially they did such a inhuman thing: they caught one of the heads of the monastery and put him on the ground with his arms and legs spread open, then he was tied with a rope to a donkey that dragged him in rounds in front of the people.

When the Chinese occupied Lhasa and tried to invite the Dalai Lama in the army camp, Tibetans surrounded Norbulingka but I was already in Lhoka. We tried to clear the way for the Dalai Lama. There were two groups: one living in Lhasa and protecting the Dalai Lama there, and my group in Lhoka helping him to get out of Tibet. The Dalai Lama escaped through Lhoka to India. Each of the army groups had to protect a part of the route through which he escaped. Since I was at the other side of Lhoka, I didn't see him. Then we also escaped but through a different road. We stayed in the border area fighting with the Chinese for a couple of days. At that time, we had some good weapons, so we could challenge them a little bit. But when we ran out of bullets, we fled to Bagsa near the border and stayed there a couple of months, from there we left for Sikkim.

We had to give our weapons to the Indian police otherwise we couldn't enter India. In Darjeeling, we worked in the road construction for one year, while the Dalai Lama was in Mussoorie. Afterwards, more than 1,000 Tibetans joined the Chushi Gangdruk and were sent to Mustang. In the beginning, we had a difficult time there; afterwards the Americans gave us support of weapons, so we could fight the Chinese sometimes. It was a guerrilla warfare, not a face to face battle.

NO 'MIDDLE WAY'

I didn't follow any training in the US, at that time I was already in Mustang. But, when those who were trained came back to Mustang, they taught us. I was not a real fighter, I had to go to the Nepalese border to observe everything and then I drew a map that was given to the leaders. Then at night, they sent thirty to forty people [to fight]. But, when I was in Tibet, I was a real fighter together with my two brothers, but my elder brother was killed by the Chinese.

In Mustang, Bawa Yeshi [big laugh] was the leader, sometimes for two or three days we had no food, but still we kept quiet and respected him. Later, he corrupted the army's salary and food. In fact he was against the Tibetans and surrendered to the Nepalese and the Chinese. Later we revolted and made a separate group.

I stayed in Mustang till 1974. Afterwards, at last we settled in Jampaling settlement. Before we had a good carpet business, we got sufficient income of it. Later, the carpet market collapsed, so now there is not much income anymore and the children have to go far from here to get a job.

When I look back on those years, there are so many sad memories: my parents, friends and family were all killed by the Chinese and even my country was occupied by them. All this I ignored, I was young and I have been fighting the Chinese and now I am old and I am still willing to fight to get my country back. But there are some people who are speaking of the 'Middle Way' or another way, but I don't like these options, I just want to fight the Chinese to get my country back.

ADVICE TO THE YOUNGER GENERATION

You have to think about the country's independence; not only the Dalai Lama but we also have to give much more effort to get our country free soon.

Interview conducted on 24 June 2007 in Jampaling.

Pemba

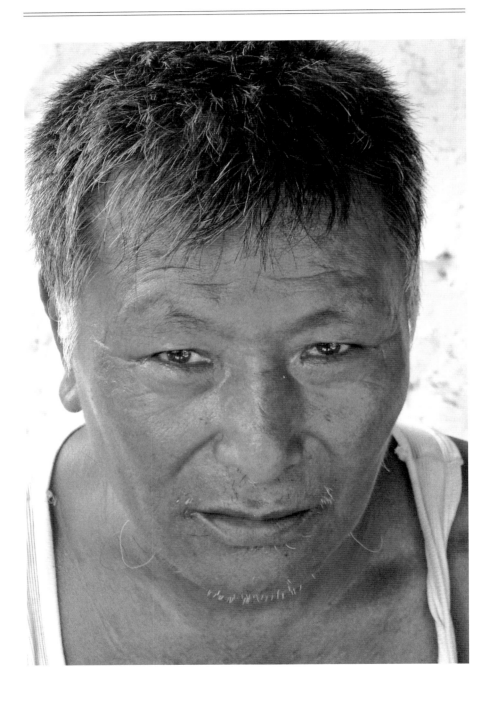

I am 63 years old and I was born in Nyam which is a place near the Nepalese-Tibetan border in the Zonga district in U-Tsang. My father's name was Dawa Dorjee, whereas my mother's name was Dawa Choedon. In my family there were five boys and five girls and we were farmers.

I don't know exactly when China occupied Tibet, I was very young at that time. But when I joined the Chushi Gangdruk, I was around seventeen years old. When I fled from Tibet, I stayed in Tsum [northern border area of Nepal]. There we got the message that if there were several sons in one family, two sons had to join the Chushi Gangdruk. So, me and my younger brother wanted to join, but due to his young age, my younger brother was not accepted. I became a member.

During the Chinese invasion, I saw lots of atrocities done to the Tibetans. Every day there was Chinese propaganda, we had to attend these meetings and listen. They explained the democratic policy and told us about the united motherland of China. But we opposed to this policy and the changes they were bringing, so we fled from Tibet.

When the Dalai Lama fled to India, I was still at home. I don't know exactly when this happened but when I heard the news, me and all the villagers of the different villages in the Zonga district fled to Lhoka and from there to Mustang. At that time, I was like twenty years old.

NO EDUCATION

My saddest memory is that, when I was young, I had no opportunity to go to school and during my stay in the army in Mustang I also didn't get the chance to get general education but only army training and training for violence. I always think that I am unlucky since I didn't get any opportunity to go to school. At that time in Mustang there was a school in Kesangbug, out of each group the two or three youngest got the chance to study there but I was already too old. I did army training all the time, only when we got holiday, we could go and see our parents.

When I knew Bawa Yeshi, he was the chief leader of the Lo-Drik-Tsug organisation. I heard that in the beginning he was a very good leader, but later when the problems started, there was a conflict and corruption between the leaders. But, I was just an ordinary soldier and I had no problems and this was only between the leaders and I only wanted to follow the guidance of the Dalai Lama.

When I stayed in Mustang, it was a happy life because we used to get guns on our shoulders and our stomach was full thanks to the support of the US; it was a happy time. After Mustang we started to build our own life: we have been digging the land and working in the fields, we have been doing handicraft and spinning the wool. But, Maoists came here and made lots of trouble; it's a very hard living for all of us Tibetans and in this country there is no life.

ADVICE TO THE YOUNGER GENERATION

These days you the youngsters, you get a very good opportunity for education and also from the parents' side they are doing big effort for this. Me and my generation, we are ignorant and, if the children are also ignorant, we cannot do anything. So you guys, take this opportunity and study and don't spoil it!

Sometimes I told my children: army life is good when you get enough food and you have nothing to worry about, but often it's very scary and very sad because you have to sacrifice your life. In fact, army is not a very good life, so I advice them to study well, then they can do any kind of job: become a teacher or work in the office and have a peaceful and comfortable life. So, I give this advice to my children.

Interview conducted on 16 June 2007 in Jampaling.

Pema Dorjee

I am 80 years old and it's in the region of Nangchen in Kham that I was born. My father passed away when I was a toddler, so I don't know his name. I don't remember my mother's name, well, in fact I do but if I tell you, then I will feel very sad, so I don't. I am the fourth child of my parents. There were seven members in my family: we were four brothers and one sister. I lived as a farmer who did an agricultural job, namely ploughing and a nomad job. Our family kept a livestock of yaks, 'dris', '*dzomos*' and sheep that could graze in places on the hill where in summer there was plenty of good grass and water. So we got milk, butter and cheese.

When I escaped from Tibet, there was one brother with me. He joined the Indian army and died in Dehradun. Do you know Rajpur? [city in India] I was living in Nepal and it was very difficult to contact him. My younger brother died in Tibet, so I never saw him again.

It was around March 1959 that the Chinese occupied Lhasa. I really don't remember exactly how old I was, that time I think I was around twenty-eight. I was a monk in the Sera monastery in Lhasa. When I left the monastery, the Chinese hadn't destroyed it yet because there were negotiations between China and Tibet to make a Tibetan autonomous area. But afterwards, they started to catch the Tibetan leaders, monks and Lamas, they destroyed the monasteries and put all the important Tibetan people in prison, they killed a number of monks and people; so I quit the monk's life.

I WAS THERE

If I speak about Mustang, I say I joined the force of Chushi Gangdruk in 1960; if I speak about Tibet, it was in 1959. I started to do freedom struggle against the Chinese troops in 1959 when the Chinese tried to lay a trap and kidnap the Dalai Lama. That was an incident around Norbulingka in Lhasa you may have heard of. Did you? [Yes] The Chinese office asked the Dalai Lama to attend a meeting. At that time he was in Norbulingka. It was doubted and suspected that the Chinese would keep the Dalai Lama in their grip once the visit was permitted. So when we came to know about this meeting, all the Tibetans came to Norbulingka and then we blocked the main gate. When we surrounded Norbulingka, we had no weapons, but we went to the storehouse of the Potala to get them.

DALAI LAMA'S SAFETY

Afterwards, the guerilla force of the Chushi Gangdruk in Lhoka escorted the Dalai Lama to safety in India through the route of Ramaga and southwards.

Tibetan people kept on gathering around Norbulingka and the Chinese troops in their turn surrounded them. I also happened to be there in people's gathering around Norbulingka. I explain you this because I was there. Otherwise, I could not have imagined all these things and have told you this.

At that time the Chinese occupied Tibet. For Tibetans and the whole world the main worry was the Dalai Lama, he is very precious. If we could protect his life, and bring him in safety, then, even if I died without seeing my parents or family, it didn't matter. When the Dalai Lama crossed the river near Norbulingka, I was there. He left with a group and I stayed in Lhasa. Chinese bombed first the Potala and then Norbulingka where trees fell down and a number of persons were killed underneath. When the Chinese got inside the Norbulingka palace by force, they killed many people: officers, monks and they were searching for the body of the Dalai Lama among them. The Chinese thought they could easily kill him, but that was not true, because the Dalai Lama was already in Lhoka.

The leader of the Chinese army told the Chinese government he had successfully captured whole Tibet. And when they asked him where the leader was, he replied the Dalai Lama was gone. So China did not win. [What was the name of this Chinese leader?] I don't remember his name, because there were so many of them.

It was in 1960 that I joined the Chushi Gangdruk in Mustang where the guerilla force unit was established. There was no way to cook for somebody, nothing to enjoy happiness, conditions were harsh: we had no mattress or blanket. We were always scared of the Chinese army coming there, we tried to destroy people and trucks and after that we got here.

YOU HAVEN'T BEEN THERE!

When I was in Mustang, Bawa Yeshi was the chief leader of the Lo-Drik-Tsug. I haven't got any picture taken in Mustang. There was no way to take pictures, you have never been there! That place is a very remote area, very cold and windy. There is not any village. Maybe people who have more education and who made maps, they maybe have some pictures. But, nobody of us had a camera or a picture.

BACK TO TIBET

In 1980, I got some news from my mother: "I am very old and if you could come and see me, please come to meet me before I die." Then, I tried and tried to go back to Tibet and see my mother. At that time, she was ninety-five and I tried to go from Nepal through Dram and tried to get the travel documents and a car, it took like twenty days and finally I reached Lhasa to meet my mother. She was sick, lying in her bed and after eight days she died. First, when I met my mother, she didn't really recognize me and touched my hand: "Are you my son...?" I was very happy to see my mother and not really upset when she died because she reached a very high age. I did Tibetan traditional praying, gave things away for the poor and donations to the monks. I spent a year and seven months in Tibet praying and offering whatever I had to the poor people and to the Lamas and monks and I visited some Buddhist holy places. I didn't face any problem since I stayed in my town and I was continuously surrounded by my friends and loved ones, but my family told me that it would be safer to leave Tibet since many people were caught by the Chinese and the situation was getting worse.

LIFE AFTERWARDS

Tell her [pointing to me] very clearly: when I arrived in Kathmandu, somebody told me I could go to Switzerland, but I didn't want because of the suffering of our peaceful land and people I wanted to take revenge on the Chinese. In the Snowland [=Tibet] from both inside and outside I hoped Tibet would come together and the Dalai Lama return back to Tibet. In that way I have spent my life till now. In Jorpati near Kathmandu, a Swiss office asked everybody to go to Switzerland, because they promised the Dalai Lama that they would help 500 Tibetans to settle in Switzerland.

In the beginning, I was doing a job in the Swiss embassy in Jwalakhel [Kathmandu]. Losang Gelek was then the representative of the Dalai Lama. I earned money, had good food and drink, but that was not my main aim. I asked to leave the office, but they didn't agree and said I should leave together with 500 Tibetans to Switzerland for resettlement. But I didn't listen to these words and ran away. I worked in this office for eleven months, but I wanted to join the Chushi Gangdruk and fight.

There is one old Tibetan story: When Buddha was on the top of a hill, his disciple was waiting near the riverside. But when Buddha returned to the riverside, his disciple had already been washed away. Similarly, for years I was waiting for the sun to rise in Tibet, but it didn't happen till now. As I am getting older and older day by day, I want Tibet to be free before I die and before I am washed away by the river.

In Tibet, I would live in happiness and peacefully, but now I am old. I am thinking of going to Tibet and live happily before I die, but now I am old, my life is finished.

ADVICE TO THE YOUNGER GENERATION

I tell this to you and you have to tell it to somebody else. Each and every individual has the responsibility to try to get back our peaceful land and bring the Dalai Lama back to the Potala. If this is not possible, then there is not any result from my advice. It would be good to have a hand-to-hand fight with the Chinese but we are only six million and they are with six billion [1,3 billion] and also most of the people in Tibet are monks just like me, who never learned to fight but studied Buddhism and practiced it.

Interview conducted on 8 June 2007 in Jampaling.

Gyurme Dorjee

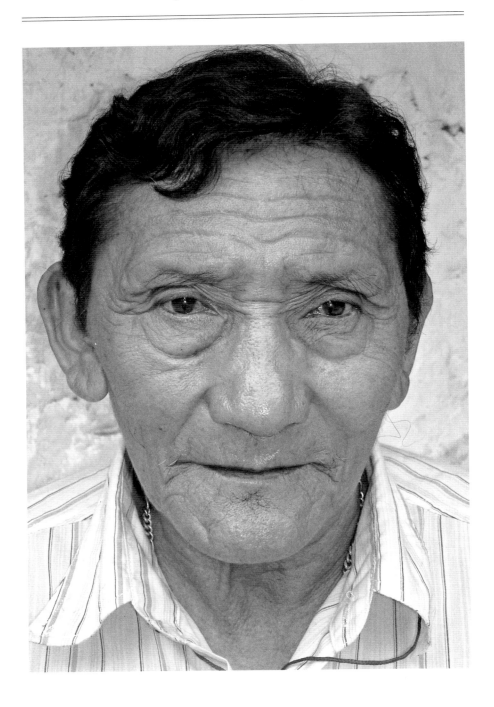

His wife passed away in 2006; he still looked very sad, and was not hearing very well.

I am 77 years old and I was born in Toe Ngari in U-Tsang. My father's name was Pema Gyantso, whereas my mother's name was Zomkyi. We were five members in our family: three brothers including me and my parents. We were nomads.

I fled to Mustang in 1959 and joined the Chushi Gangdruk in 1963. I was not along with the Dalai Lama when he fled to India, because he left from Lhasa to India. At that time, the Chinese were not yet in our village, but later they were and gave money and food and were very friendly. They tried to cheat us telling the government of Lhasa was not good and they tried to corrupt the people of the village, saying the Tibetan government was feudal and every day they made propaganda to follow them.

WORKING AS A DOCTOR

Then, I ran away from Tibet to Mustang, it was not far from where I lived. Many people followed each other to escape to Mustang and to India. In our village at that time we were not fighting the Chinese, but they were already occupying the other side of Tibet.

Being a Tibetan doctor, I was ordered by the leader to take care of the patients who, due to the different weather, suffered from swollen, painful feet and legs, because Tibet is cold and Mustang is hot. So these were not caused by long walking but by the difference in altitude. There were sixty patients with these problems. In my clinic, I also took care of the patients who had problems due to the different water and the lack of food. Some of them had ear problems too and could hardly hear. Since we were staying there for a long time and we had no good food to eat, there were more and more diseases. For me, the climate in Tibet and Mustang was similar, because Mustang is situated only a little lower than the place where I come from.

During the fourteen years I was only looking after the patients, so I didn't know how to fight or to be a guerrilla. I saw Bawa Yeshi, but I never had a conversation with him. While I stayed in Mustang, I just looked after the patients. I was the Tibetan doctor and there was also a western doctor, that was a Tibetan who studied western medicine. So there was not much opportunity to meet Bawa Yeshi and I cannot tell anything about him. The other Tibetan doctors, I think they already died.

I was in Mustang from 1963 till 1974. Afterwards, we were in Nuwakot and we stayed there for one year. We were sent by groups to Nuwakot jail. I was in the tenth group. In Nuwakot, the situation was not so bad: we were given food but we were not free to go where we wanted. In this prison we were playing games and cards and praying, reciting "Om mani padme hum", and sometimes we had to go out and pick up the firewood.[1] For almost fourteen years, we have been working very hard for the Lo-Drik-Tsug; in the meantime the Nepalese government destroyed the army base. Then, we had to make a new life again and it was difficult to find accommodation to live and since we had lots of children, it gave extra problems. Afterwards, we received help from the Tibetan government and support from foreigners who started to build a school. Then, our situation improved and our children got the opportunity to go to school and study.

Later, I went to 'Tenshug' in Dharamsala. When the Dalai Lama asked me where I came from, I told him I was from U-Tsang and that I was a doctor in Mustang. He only replied that this was good. Since there were lots of people, he didn't say more and I had to leave.

ADVICE TO THE YOUNGER GENERATION

I have not much advice to give, only that they need to keep our culture alive and need to study, especially in this century, it is very important to study science.

Interview conducted on 2 July 2007 in Jampaling.

Takhor

I am 85 years old and I don't know my place of birth or my father's or mother's name because when I was small a Chinese took me to Tehor and I lived with him. He claimed to be a relative, but I don't know if we were or not. He told me I was his son but he was exploiting me. So I ran away and stayed with a Tibetan family and looked after the animals. When I grew up, this family that had many horses, gave me some job to do. One time I had to go to Lhasa with twenty horses to do some tea business. I was almost twenty at that time, but the situation in Lhasa deteriorated and so I couldn't go back and joined the Chushi Gangdruk. I sent the horses with the goods back home through someone else.

I voluntarily joined and the leader was Andrug Gompo Tashi. We stayed in Lhoka and I fought with the Chinese many times.

I came to India and reached first in Misamari, there I handed over all the weapons I had and went to Kalimpong. My story is the same as Lobsang Dorjee's [next interview]; we lived the same experience, but I don't remember much due to my high age. I also did the road working job and after 1960 I joined in Mustang and I stayed there with my friends till 1974. You can ask anyone about what I am telling you, my story is very true.

I don't know the year when I arrived in Tashigang, but it was when the gompa and some other buildings were already finished. I worked in a carpet factory, but now I am a retired staff and I receive money from the Lo-Drik-Tsug.

ADVICE TO THE YOUNGER GENERATION

I am an uneducated person, so I cannot give this kind of advice for the younger generation. The only thing is to read books very carefully and study hard. What I have told you today, is true.

Interview conducted on 26 June 2007 in Tashigang.

Lobsang Dorjee

I am 83 years old and I was born in Gyantse in U-Tsang region. My father's name was Gyalpo whereas my mother's name was Dolma. I had three sisters and two brothers, so seven family members and I was the youngest. I was a monk in Tibet in Gyantse monastery with about 2,000 other monks divided in sixteen groups.

I think it was in 1957 [1958] when the Chushi Gangdruk was founded in Lhoka; from my monastery 200 monks wanted to join voluntarily this organization, but it was so difficult to go there in one group because at that time Gyantse was already invaded by the Chinese. So, I joined the Chushi Gangdruk in 1958 in Lhoka with a group of twenty monks. We prepared the way for the Dalai Lama to India. My group was in Lhoka in Chusum and the leader Gompo Tashi was not there; they were on their way to the Gaden Choekhor monastery to get some weapons. But, they had problems to come back because they had to fight lots of Chinese on the way, so instead they went to Jhang. At that time, we had two other leaders, Amdo Lhaksey and Minag Gompo, and I stayed with them about one year.

FLEEING THROUGH BHUTAN

After one year in Drikuthang, there were some soldiers from Derge monastery and some of the Gaden Choekhor monastery and for five days we fought against 2,000 Chinese. One of my friends had a machine gun and we carried it. On the way, twelve of our members were injured and also four of my friends were killed just in front of me. We also killed many Chinese but I don't know the exact number. Then, we tried to reach our house and food supplies, but since the area was already occupied by the Chinese, it was impossible to get back to the army camp, so we ran away with just our guns.

We escaped to India but at the border of Bhutan there were lots of children, laymen and old people waiting since more than one month, because the Bhutanese government didn't allow them to enter. They were waiting for some news from India. When I reached the border, after four days the Indian government accepted the Dalai Lama and his people, then only Bhutan allowed us to enter. But we couldn't follow the normal road, we had to go through the mountains, up and down, it was so difficult. Some villagers gave us food. For us, it wasn't too difficult because we were young, but there were lots of children, old people and women who faced lots of problems on the way. Finally, we reached the Indian border, namely Bagsa, it used to be a prison of the English. We stayed there for two months. Most of the people had their own family and there were also some soldiers and monks and then they sent us to Gangtok and we worked on the road for one year.

In 1960, I went to Mustang to be a guerrilla fighter and during that time I didn't get the chance to fight the Chinese, most of the time I was working for

Road workers. (*TibetMuseum/ DIIR*)

the group and giving assistance to the leaders and I was a cashier accountant until 1974. But of course our group and the leader Ragra, they went to Tibet and killed Chinese and destroyed the jeep, they made such great history.

In 1974, I came to Pokhara to work with Mr Wangyal (interview 1) and worked as a cashier of the carpet factory and later also in Kathmandu. At that time I did my job in a good way and most of the people appreciated my work. Then I got an ear problem and underwent an operation, I retired and now I am here.

PENSION

I know a little bit about Bawa Yeshi. So, that time he didn't keep the accounts clearly. Most of the soldiers were against him and we always kept an eye on him but our leaders Gen Wangdu and Lhamo Tsering told us that there was no problem with the finances, then we just left him alone. Later, Bawa Yeshi and his group went down to Pokhara and surrendered to the Nepalese government and he made a group from the people of Batang county, he took them with him to Katmandu and he got a small piece of land in Jorpati [place at the outskirts of Kathmandu].

Some of his group are living near the Indian border in Lumbini, I don't know where exactly. But when we met, they told us it was very hot and the conditions were very poor, but I never went there myself. Some of them stayed in Trishuli, so I was thinking they were so rich because Bawa Yeshi took enough money for them. So now I am old, so I don't have any income from work, I depend on the pension from the Lo-Drik-Tsug office.

ADVICE TO THE YOUNGER GENERATION

I don't have any education, I told already what I did in Tibet and Mustang, that's all I did voluntarily for the independence of Tibet. As I know, this is also the responsibility for every single Tibetan. The younger generation has modern education, so they know everything, so I cannot give them advice since compared to them, I am less educated.

Interview conducted on 26 June 2007 in Tashigang.

Tsering

I am 79 years old [he looks much younger] and I was born in Narthang, in the region of U-Tsang. My father's name was Tsering and my mother's name was Pempa. In my family we were nine members, four sisters and two brothers, and father and mother. Our occupation in Tibet was agriculture.

In 1959, I joined the Chushi Gangdruk in Drikuthang, I was thirty-one years old. I didn't get the chance to fight the Chinese when I was in Tibet; sometimes we did only a small fighting, but no serious fight. With a group we escaped to India, to Montawang to Sikkim and Darjeeling. We worked on the road construction in Gangtok for one year.

Then, in 1960 Chushi Gangdruk restarted to collect people and I also joined them and went to Mustang in Nepal. In the first year, we had a food problem and the facilities were very bad. The second year, we got training how to fight guerrilla and in 1961, we got weapons from the airplane; the first time, they threw the weapons in Lektse Tsongra, that's the border of Tibet.

LOST IN THE FOG

We were fourteen groups, and the weapons were given to eight of them. The second time the other groups also got weapons. First, 400 people were sent to the border, lived there and learned how to enter Tibet. From that group, 100 soldiers were separated and also four teachers: Tsering Dorjee, Kelsang, Ragra and Gyaltsen, and four other leaders went to fight, namely Wangdu, Chamdo Tsepa, Tenzin, and Asang. We went to one of the two Chinese army camps. We were five people to go to Drakgyawu and we met eight or nine Chinese soldiers who were there near the border; we killed them all. In fact, we were not planning to fight them, but we met them and just killed them. Our leader sent me back to Mustang to report the details from the border, but that time it was very difficult to go back because of the fog, so I got lost. I walked non-stop for three days and still I didn't reach Mustang, even worse, I arrived near the Chinese army camp again. Then I hid and searched for the road and some of my colleagues saw me and thought I was a Chinese. Because it was difficult to recognize me, they almost killed me! Later, it became foggy again, so nobody could see me anymore and I continued my way. Then I finally reached the army camp and reported everything. Later, our financial army situation was getting better and we bought many horses and became horse fighters.

I went a couple of times to Tibet to bomb the road and also the trucks [laughing and gesturing expressively while explaining]. One time, we attacked a truck and killed eleven soldiers and took all their weapons. Most of the time we put bombs and damaged the roads. Each time different soldiers were sent by our leader, he chose twenty people to go to the border, depending on the needs. After that, lots of Chinese came to the border and it became impossible to fight them face to face, but still we tried to do guerrilla attacks. In 1974, the Nepalese government sent the Nepalese army to Mustang to get all the Tibetan arms but we really didn't want to give them; we really wanted to fight both of them [the Chinese and the Nepalese]. But, the Dalai Lama sent a message to our army camp and then we listened to him and we gave all the weapons back; after that we were powerless.

After Mustang, we came to Pokhara to build the Annapurna hotel until it was finished. In fact, I still cannot speak very good Nepali.

ADVICE TO THE YOUNGER GENERATION

I have four children and I always tell them to learn how to fight and that when they get the chance, they have to go to China and fight the Chinese if they can. Other young people have to do the same and study very hard and try to get training to fight the Chinese. One of my sons is in the Indian army now, so he is already prepared to be a fighter.

Interview conducted on 19 June 2007 in Paljorling.

Yeshi Sherab

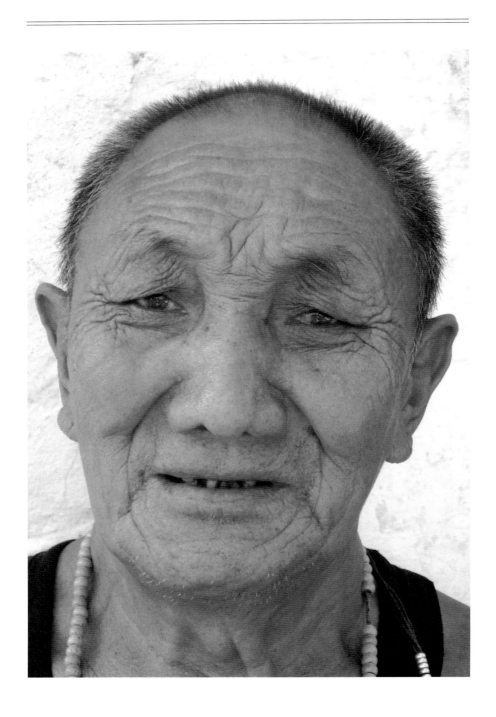

While telling his story, he pointed out with his finger, as if he were telling a story to his children; the interviewer was indeed his granddaughter.

I am 73 years old and I was born in Gyalrong Tsenlha, it's in Amdo, Eastern Tibet, near the border of China [not so far from Chengdu]. My father's name was Namgyal, whereas my mother's name was Dorjee. In my family were nine members: father, mother, grandmother, one brother and four sisters. Our occupation was agriculture.

SPECIAL GUYS

In 1959, I was twenty-five years old, I was in Tibet and joined the Chushi Gangdruk. There were three different groups, I stayed in Lhoka Tsetang, so we had to prepare the way for the escape of the Dalai Lama. When the people surrounded Norbulingka, our group was responsible to fight the Chinese in Lhoka, so I couldn't join the Dalai Lama to escape. At that time our weapons were very bad, we had to put the bullets one by one. Of course we are very special guys, since we helped the Dalai Lama to escape safely.

When we were in Lhoka, we were not fighting all the time, but sometimes it was very heavy; many Chinese were killed and they also killed some members of our group.

When the Dalai Lama escaped to India, we protected the local people who were also escaping. Then, unfortunately because we were outnumbered by the Chinese, we couldn't cope with them; and above all we had no good weapons, so we escaped to Magola in India. Then to Misamari, there it was very hot and difficult to live, that's why we asked to be sent to another place. The Indian government divided us and sent a group to Assam and one to Bomdila, so there we worked on the road construction for one year.

MAKING HISTORY

After a couple of months, we felt so bored and sad that we were working for India, and so in 1960 the Tibetan government organised the Chushi Gangdruk and sent us to Mustang. Nobody was forced, we went voluntarily. We stayed there till 1974. Most of the time we did guerrilla fighting, so nobody could see us. In the beginning it was a very difficult life with lots of food problems. We boiled the yak skin, and many people were sick. After that the American government supported us and our situation improved. But unfortunately in 1974, the Nepalese government launched a crackdown on us but most of our members wanted to fight. Then, we received the Dalai

Lama's message and after hearing the message, we gave all the weapons to the Nepalese.

During fourteen years we only thought about our country, there was not any individual benefit, so that's why the Tibetan government and the Dalai Lama feel more close to us. We couldn't make that much history for our country, but we did our best.

First, Bawa Yeshi was the main leader in Mustang, but after a few years Gen Wangdu became our leader. Then between them, there was some problem, but I don't know clearly what was the reason behind, I was just an ordinary soldier, so I cannot tell you the full story.

Some people were sent to US to get training and when they came back, they taught us guerilla fighting and map reading. During fourteen years, I often went to Tibet, but I don't know if I killed any Chinese or not.

After Mustang, we came down [to Pokhara] and had a problem with the language and the food, but for the rest there were not so many problems because the Tibetan government supported us as much as they could, so our life was not that difficult in Nepal.

ADVICE TO THE YOUNGER GENERATION

I don't have any education, so I don't know how to give any advice. And also the youngsters do not listen to people without any education like me.

Interview conducted on 19 June 2007 in Paljorling.

Lobsang Tsering

I am 68 years old and I was born in the region of Toe, namely in the village Lungring in the province of U-Tsang. My father's name was Dawa but my mother already died long time ago, so I don't remember her name. I had nine members in my family, four brothers and me, and two sisters who got married and lived in another place and had their own house. Our occupation was nomad, I watched the grazing animals: sheep, yaks, horses that belonged to the monastery because I had to pay taxes to the monastery and to the Depa Shung [= name used in earlier times to designate the Tibetan government]. At that time, we had no school or no place where we could get education or technology, we couldn't learn anything.

PAYING TAXES

When the Chinese came, I saw them only from far away, but they didn't come in Toe or occupy my village because we were living in the mountains. But we heard Lhasa and also the lower regions of Kham were already occupied by them. After that, whole Tibet was occupied and we all had difficulties with living without food. We heard the Dalai Lama escaped to India and many Tibetans after him to safe their life. Other Tibetans fled from their area and came without their belongings or animals to Toe, to places near the border like Tarom* and Lekshe because this region was not yet occupied. We didn't suffer the same fate as other people because we didn't have to leave our belongings and everything behind. I haven't seen any atrocities done by the Chinese, like killings or separating children from their parents. I haven't had any face to face contact with them.

My father had also no problem with the Chinese but during that time he was not paying taxes to the Depa Shung, and so Dasang Sonam Tsering and his colleagues beat him up and tortured him. He came back with a broken arm and died after three days.

My two elder brothers joined the Chushi Gangdruk in Yarabug, my elder sister died. Two orders came from the government and also people came to our home to convince everybody to join the army, so I joined. All the people who were working as house servants also joined. We, the people from Toe, came with all our belongings straight to Mustang, while others went first to India before coming to Mustang.

I joined the Chushi Gangdruk in Mustang; I don't know exactly in which year of the modern calendar but it must have been around 1962. I was engaged in the duty of patrolling and spying, with binoculars I saw Chinese on horses, soldiers by foot and army trucks, but I only saw them from far, from the top of the mountains.

I didn't kill any Chinese, I was only a spy and watched the Chinese approaching. I never got any training, also not in the US. I was like a guard or storekeeper to look after the animals and the weapons.

I came to know about the Dalai Lama fleeing to India when I was in Mustang. During my stay there I remember we sometimes had problems of food, but I still enjoyed a lot and I was always happy to be there. As a soldier, we had the difficult task to climb the mountains during the night. We mostly went at night to the border and it was hard to see the way since we were not allowed to use a candle light or take a torch. Sometimes it took two to three days, and we were about ten groups of soldiers, sometimes more or less, it depended on the situation. We couldn't make any noise. We had to climb very high, so we were surrounded by the clouds and sometimes it was so foggy that it was difficult to see the way, it was cold and there was snow and we couldn't see any direction, north or south, and at night it was even more difficult. But, Amdo Samdup and the instructors knew how to use the compass and told us where to go.

In 1974, when soldiers were sent to Nuwakot, I was not there. I was still in Mustang selling the sheep, yaks and clothes of the Chushi Gangdruk's soldiers. We were three to do this work: me together with Yadung Choeze and Shawong Yonten. These two had the right to sell all these things to the local peoples and later they used the money for themselves because there was nobody to hand over the money. A few years later they passed away.

Lobsang Tsering with his daughter Nangsa Choedon.

Bawa Yeshi was the leader of the Chushi Gangdruk, there was a problem between him and the Tibetan government. Due to that, the soldiers were split in two groups and later Bawa Yeshe chose the Nepalese government's side. Then they asked to hand over the weapons to them and after that the situation went worse. Later the soldiers were given papers and were sent to Nuwakot, then to Kotre Khola, and from there to the Jampaling settlement.

When I arrived in Jampaling there were only bamboo houses and small huts, no monastery, no houses. At that time I met again Yadung Choeze and Shawong Yonten.

Right now, I have a difficult life but I can still work; I can see and work and still have energy. I am not blind but if I get any physical problem, then I have to seek help from the government and then I will go to the old people's home.

ADVICE TO THE YOUNGER GENERATION

I am not so happy with the youngsters of today. I came from a poor nomad family, so what can I advice them since I have no education? They have to study hard and should run their life happily and it should be good to study. For the present youngsters they are very fortunate that the Dalai Lama is there to give advice and they should follow it. When we were in Tibet, we couldn't see him. Even if we are living in exile, they get a wonderful chance to study, so don't waste your time. It's an important chance that they have to take. This is my simple advice.

Interview conducted on 24 June 2007 in Jampaling.

Tsering Siten

Since November 2007, he is the Settlement Officer of the settlements of Jampaling, Paljorling and Tashigang in Pokhara.

I am 55 years old. I am from Lekshe, in U-Tsang. My father's name was Lobsang Choepel and my mother's name was Samchung. We were nomads and I had only four family members: father, mother, me and my younger brother.

I joined the Chushi Gangdruk in 1963 in Mustang, they had arrived there in 1961. My father was already a member of this organisation. My situation was very sad: my mother died in the early sixties and afterwards my younger brother also died. The cause of my brother's dead was that he died on the road when we escaped from Tibet, due to the heavy snow; he was only four. And so my father joined the Chushi Gangdruk and I also joined it. Before I joined, I lived with my relatives.

In the sixties when I was very young, lots of children were sent to India [to go to school]. But my father who heard that many of them died due to the hot weather, was worried about me, so he kept me with him and didn't send me to school.

When we were in Tibet, normally in Lekshe and as a nomad we didn't face any trouble from the Chinese. I only came to know about the Dalai Lama's escape after a long time.

ONLY ELEVEN YEARS OLD

I joined Chushi Gangdruk when I was almost eleven years old. I didn't have to do military activities, but I did cattle rearing for the Lo-Drik-Tsug. First, I was given the job of courier, like a postman I had to bring the post to different areas. I had to walk many miles, I was running very fast.

Tsering Siten in 1967. (*Collection of Tsering Siten*)

In Mustang, they opened a school for the young soldiers, so I joined that school for two years and there we were taught Tibetan as main subject, the English ABC, mathematics and map reading. After that school, I got a job in one group in which I had to do the accounting, because at that time there were few people who could do that job. I continued that job and later I got a job in the first office of the seventh group in which I got more responsibility: I distributed clothes, ration, etc. to the different groups, and I was also responsible for the arrangement of sending horses and mules to the border area to infiltrate in Tibet. In total there were sixteen groups; the distance between them was two days walk [he shows on the map where the different groups were situated]. My group counted like 100 people and each had five administrative workers who did the whole administration. I continued this job till 1974.

In 1974, when the Nepalese government ordered to surrender the arms, I felt that we should use these arms against them; I was very excited to use these new weapons because we had been keeping them for years. I was young at that time, so I was very curious to use them, they were very nice and we had never used them. I was not worried about my own future, I was really motivated to fight. At that time, some senior members were saying that we had better arms than the Nepalese and that they couldn't overpower us and that the Chinese would naturally come and help them and so this would be a good opportunity to fight the Chinese. So we were not really motivated to give back these weapons.

In previous times, in the eighteenth century, Mustang was a part of Tibet. The Mustang people didn't speak Nepali, they spoke Tibetan and had the same face. In the sixties when we first came, there was no Nepalese police, only one Indian radio signal man. It was a very isolated area. Nepal was very poor at that time, so there was an Indian telegrapher. Maybe he was spying on the Chinese activities in the border area after the Chinese occupation of Tibet?

I remember around 1962 the Chinese and Nepalese built up a small cemented boundary stone, one side was written in Chinese and the other in Nepalese language and that was the border mark between the two countries; it was a small one. When I was small, I used to rear the cattle in that area and I used to throw stones on this stone but I didn't damage it.

UNDER OATH

I knew Bawa Yeshi. In 1963, when I joined Chushi Gangdruk, there was an Amdo leader Jangchuk Jimpa; his assistant called us inside a tent where there was a portrait of the Dalai Lama. Mr Jangchuk told us: "You can bring information from outside but you cannot speak about our activities outside, and you have to make an oath in front of the picture of the Dalai Lama". After two years, we came to learn that Bawa Yeshi was coming to visit us and we got a khaki uniform and we washed it and made ourselves look tidy. So we were ready to receive him standing in a line and Bawa Yeshi gave some lectures: "You all should keep your moral high and get ready and in two or three years Tibet will get its independence back". He talked a lot but I don't remember much. That time I believed this speech very much. He gave us a small present, small multicoloured towels and a red soap. I was very happy with my towel and I used to hang it over my neck. When I was in school in Kesangbug, Bawa Yeshi often used to visit us with five guards and dogs.

After 1974, all the people went to settle in the area of Pokhara and me with five men were left behind, we had to finish everything: sell the things etc. When I came to Pokhara, the officials of the Tibetan government-in-exile came to Pokhara and I informed them about the accounts. Then I was sent as one of the first to Jampaling settlement, during that time the young Lo-Drik-Tsug soldiers were also sent to Dehradun for the Indian army. So I had given my name but my name didn't come and I was left alone, all the others went to Dehradun. I was in doubt and later the secretary Lobsang Tsultrim told me that I had to go and study dyeing [colouring the wool for carpets] for the handicraft and I was asked to follow that course and I know that they deliberately didn't send me to Dehradun. Although I was not satisfied with this job and I didn't want to stay in that place, I continued because I remembered the speech of the Dalai Lama: "You all should stay together in unity and work hard". Wherever I went, anyway I was living on a foreign soil and there was no difference, that speech encouraged me to stay in Jampaling.

ADVICE TO THE YOUNGER GENERATION

The present youngsters have a lot of opportunities for education, very nice opportunities, not as in previous times. So they must take them. During our time, we didn't have those facilities to go to school, even if I learned the Tibetan language. Going for education is not only for doing office work, they should be able to do any kind of work. During the sixties when the Tibetans came here, the Tibetan government-in-exile needed a lot of English translators and interpreters, so many tried to do these jobs. Now at present there are enough people to do these jobs, now it is time that youngsters study in other fields like agriculture and technology which are very much necessary for the future nation building.

Interview conducted on 27 June 2007 in the Lo-Drik-Tsug Office in Pokhara. Tsering Siten lives in Tashigang settlement.

Ngawang Tsultrim

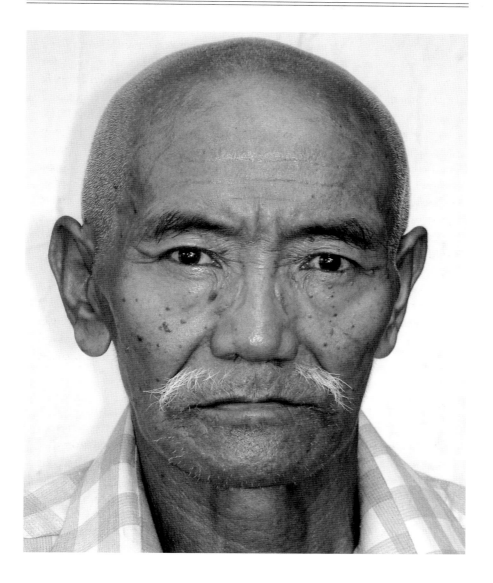

I am 73 years old and I was born in Dakpo, in U-Tsang. My father's name was Sonam Wangpo and my mother's name was Choedon. I have the same father and the same mother as my only sister. She is younger and is living now in Medok Gonkar [Institute of Buddhist Dialectics and Monastery near

Lhasa]. In my childhood, my parents sent me to a small monastery in Dakpo to become a monk. My mother was from Lhasa and lots of relatives were living there, so I went to Lhasa and I entered the Ganden monastery. Our family were farmers, my father looked after the animals and my mother used to work in the field.

In 1958, when I was in Ganden, the Chinese didn't use violence in Lhasa, but we heard they damaged and killed people in Kham and Amdo. In 1959, before the Chinese completely attacked Lhasa, Ganden was not yet destroyed. During the time of offering a Geshe degree to the Dalai Lama in the Drepung monastery, the Chinese controlled Ganden and Drepung and made lots of problems everywhere in Lhasa. For his examination, the Dalai Lama attended a Buddhist ceremony in the three monasteries: Sera, Drepung and Ganden and that time the Chinese invited him for a party. Many Geshes had been invited before to their office and never returned, so people thought this was a bad sign and came to surround Norbulingka.

Fortunately, one night the Dalai Lama left and went to Dranang. A few days after the people surrounded Norbulingka and protected the Dalai Lama, the Chinese destroyed Lhasa, used bombs and destroyed the monasteries.

I felt anger and was scared at the same time and so I felt I had been monk for a long time, and thought the best way to protect the Dalai Lama and save his life, was to join the army. I thought it would be something honourable and that's why in 1959 I joined the army in Lhoka. I was not with him when he escaped to India, but we protected him and checked if everything was safe on the way from Lhasa to Gongkar and then to Dranang, which took one day and a half. In Dranang he wore lay dress and advised us, a group of fifty soldiers, to return back to Lhasa to guard the Lhasa people.

I joined the Chushi Gangdruk for several reasons. We had to make a promise not to steal anything or do corruption or robbery and protect the people against the Chinese enemy and dedicate our life to the nation in particular. The rules were very strict. I still keep this memory in my heart: the day I joined the army I was full of enthusiasm and love or reverence to the nation. I joined the army with sheer dedication and the philosophy of "to do or die".

SPYING AND ANNOYING THE CHINESE

In 1959, [we fled from Tibet] and stayed in Misamari, but we had never the dream of staying there: our only plan was to go back. We worked in Gangtok for about one year, like ten months, in the road construction. At that time, there was a rumour about a new army station in Mustang. So I decided again, as when I was in Tibet, to join the army, so I left for Mustang.

With the new army station and the training for guerrilla fighter, maybe there would be a possibility to get our country back. Due to my young age, I was not among the members to go to America for training, but I know somebody who did and came to Mustang and became a leader.

During our stay there until 1974, we had a hard time: we did training and went into Tibet to spy upon the Chinese; a couple of Tibetan soldiers even lost their lives. We lived in Nepal, crossed the border of Tibet and fought from time to time. We were not a real army, but guerrilla fighters and we went quietly off and on; the main purpose was to annoy the Chinese.

We could never relax and also during the night we kept all our clothes. We used a stone as a pillow and the ground as a bed. There was no possibility to wander around, we had to stay in the same place: on the top of the hill, day and night.

There was also lack of food and the facilities were very poor. We hardly ate a complete meal in a day because food was scarce. When the leaders asked us if we were hungry, we never said yes, because we had already decided to be real soldiers and we were ready to give our lives for our country. Thanks to the American support the conditions got better. I have no photos of my life in Mustang, but I know the army office has some.

The main thing is that the exile is very long and you [western] people, you support us to keep up our Tibetan culture and political views. So, I would like to say to you: "Thank you very much".

ADVICE TO THE YOUNGER GENERATION

For the Tibetans, I want to share this with all the Tibetan youngsters: don't do negative things, be true, never cheat and always tell the truth, study hard and respect old people and keep love between parents and kids, have mutual respect and get back our country, that is my request.

I think already forty to fifty years have passed to get our freedom back and I am always thinking Tibetans have to be united like milk and water that mix, that is the only wish and prayer I have. My life is going by over here and by the grace of the Dalai Lama I can stay here. I want to dedicate my life to my country and to him but I am worried about when I can go back. About China and Tibet, the Chinese seem to ignore the Dalai Lama's approach, maybe because they have the money and the power. So I ask to all the nations to give support for the peace talk with the Chinese so that the Dalai Lama could go back to Tibet and Tibetans could live as real Tibetans in Tibet. That is my main effort and goal.

Interview conducted on 10 June 2007 in Jampaling.

Dhondup Tsering

I am 65 years old and I was born in Tewa in Toe, U-Tsang. My father's name was Sonam Tenzin while my mother's was Yumtso. There were ten children in my family, but they all passed away at young age except for my elder sister and me. We were nomads, we had yaks, sheep and goats and we made cheese and butter for selling.

I joined the Chushi Gangdruk in Mustang when I was eighteen. When we had heard that the Chinese were coming, I fled with my parents, my elder sister had already died in the meantime, and some villagers. We left with forty yaks and some 100 sheep and goats. We rode on our yaks till Lo-Monthang, but there was not enough food for them on the way, no grass, so some of them died. Others were taken by villagers when the animals came on their fields. All our belongings were also carried by the yaks. Afterwards we had to continue by foot till Muktinath. My father expired in Zar, there was no village and I had to take his body on my back. One friend, Thewa Lama helped me to give the body to the vultures, but we didn't have the opportunity to do prayers or offerings or call a Lama [= to do the usual funeral rituals]. Afterwards, my mother and I went for pilgrimage by foot to Kathmandu through a small village Marak*, it took us one month. Then we returned to Manang and to Muktinath, there I joined the army and was separated from my mother. I didn't see her for five or six years and came to know she was living in Jawalakhel [Tibetan refugee camp in Kathmandu].

I didn't really fight, I was a spy at the border. I got training from those who went to the US. We didn't decide for ourselves, we got the order to go either in the morning or in the evening. There were fifteen groups of 100 soldiers and two groups went to spy, turn by turn. The leader decided where we had to go; I had to go to the border of Dolpo, because at the other side of the hill, in Tibet was a Chinese army cantonment. We had to look if they were planning to attack; we stayed there for two months if the situation was tense, otherwise only for one month. Next to this, we also had to look after the guns and weapons storeroom.

[Were you there when they faced food problems?] I wasn't there; our main food was maize 'thukpa' and we got a ration of a half kg of tsampa for one week and as a salary we were given a half kg of rice. I sold this to the Mustang villagers to buy dry vegetables.

At that time, we received support from the US for weapons but I never saw that they were dropped by airplanes. Ahnzin [interview 5] and Lobsang Monlam [interview 18] were also in my group.

SNOW BLINDNESS

My greatest sufferings were that even when we were sick, we couldn't decide for ourselves not to go and spy. And also on the way from Tibet I suffered from snow blindness and in Mustang my eyes pained a lot and even till now it still affects me.

Moreover, I regret a lot that I never had the chance to go and study, without education life is very difficult.

Before the occupation I had such a happy life in Tibet, but after the Chinese invasion there were so many problems on the way and also my father died. Till I joined the Chushi Gangdruk, then my situation improved a little bit. It's hard to express my deep feelings with words, but this is what I remember the most.

AFRAID TO JUMP

I stayed in Mustang for eleven years. Then, there was this war between India and Bangladesh and most of the young men were sent to India.[1] I also went there, I stayed in Dehradun, but I didn't have to fight; they have been sending the elder ones. I got training for five years. I also learned to jump from an airplane. The first time I fainted, I was so afraid, we were pushed in the back to jump, we couldn't refuse. My whole body shivered, afterwards when my parachute opened, I was so relieved. We only jumped when there was no wind, three times in the morning, three times in the evening; it was so high! I never jumped in Mustang, but we just learnt it in case it would be useful.

When the Nepalese army sent the soldiers to Nuwakot, I was not there. At that time, I was called back from India, but I wasn't able to reach Mustang. So I stayed in Pokhara for two months, then I went to Kotre Kohla and finally to Jampaling.

ADVICE TO THE YOUNGER GENERATION

While I was in Mustang, I didn't get the chance to study, we just struggled with our body, there was no learning. In this twenty-first century, education is most important, so youngsters should give full effort to study.

Interview conducted on 28 February 2009 in Jampaling.

EPILOGUE

I conclude my will by praying for the full success of our cause under the leadership of His Holiness the Dalai Lama. Judging from past history, I know that the world changes fast and no situation remains static. I assure you that the day is not far off when you will again be able to set your feet on the sacred land of Tibet.

Excerpt from the will of Andrug Gompo Tashi, leader of the Chushi Gangdruk

APPENDIX 1

ANTHEM OF THE UPRISING

ཡེ་ལ་ལ་ཕྱུག་ནི་ཚོན།
ཡོ་པ་འཕྲོག །
ཡེ་ལོ་འཆུ་ཕྱུག་ལ་རུ། །ལ་ཚོ་ལོ། །
ནུ་ཇུ་རུ་པ་ལ་ལ་ཟན་ལ་རུ། །
ཁུ་འོ་པ་འཆག་ན་ནོ་ཀ་ན་རུ་ལ་ཁེ། །
ཆེ་ག་རོ་ལུ་ལ་རྒྱུ་ལ་རྐྱུ་ལ་ལ་ནི་ལོ་ཟ། །
རྒྱ་ལ་ནཆ་པ་ལ་ལ་ལ་ཟན་ལ་འོ་ལེ་ལ་ཟ་པ་ལ་ཀྱེ་པ། །
ནེ་ག་ལ་རུ་རུ་ལ་ལ་པ་ལོ། །
ཡོ་པ་འཕྲོག་ལོ་པ་འཕྲོག་ལ་ཚི་ལོ་འཕྲུ་པ། །
འཇའ་ལ་ནེ་ལོ་ལ་ལ་ཚི་ག་ཅུ་ར་ལོ་པ་འཕྲོག །
ནེ་ག་པ་ནི་པ་ལོ་ལ་རྗེ་ལ་ཉེ། །
ཟོ་ལ་རྫོ་པ་ལ་ག་ལ་ནི་རུ་ཉི་ལ། །
ཨྞྞ་ཟ་པ་ལ་ནོ་ག་ན་ལོ། །
ནོ་ལ་པ་ལེ་འཆི་ག་ན་རོ་རུ། །
ག་ཞི་པ་ཟ་པ་ཙོ་ལ་ལོ་ནེ་ཚོ་ད་རྗེ་ད། །
ཁུ་འོ་ལེ་ཟ་ག་ལ་ལ་ག་ལ་པ་ཟ། །
འཚང་ག་རྒྱ་ལ་ཇ་ལོ་ནི་ལ་པ་ལ་ཟ་རུ་ཙོ་ལ་ཀྱོ་ལེ་ལེ་ག །
རྒྱ་ལ་ནཆ་པ་ལ་ཡེ་ལ་ལ་ཡོ་པ་འཕྲོག །

Rise up! For ten long years,
Persecuted by our enemy,
our very flesh torn from the bone!
persecuted by the enemy,
our very flesh torn from the bone!

In 1959, in desperation the people of Tibet
rose up for truth and justice.
In desperation the people of Tibet
rose up for truth and justice.

Rise up, rise up, you who love Tibet,
Rise up, rise up, you people of the world;
Support us, hear our cries for justice!
Rise up, rise up, you people of the world;
Support us, hear our cries for justice!

Protector of Tibet, His Holiness the Dalai Lama,
only true leader of Tibetans everywhere.
His Holiness the Dalai Lama,
only true leader of Tibetans everywhere.

Oh enemy with butcher's bloody hands,
Murderous red Chinese,
We are going to drive you from Tibet!
Rise up, all you who love Tibet!

(Both anthems taken from: *Incomparable Warriors. Non-violent Resistance in Contemporary Tibet.* ICT, 2005, p. 4.)

LONG LIFE PRAYER FOR HIS HOLINESS THE DALAI LAMA

OM SVASTI

Rab jam gyal wa'i sang sum ma lü pa
Gang dul chir yang char wa'i gyu trul gar
Srid sh'i ge leg kun jung yid shin nor
Ngo gyud drin chän la ma'i tsog nam la

Dag chag dung shug drag pö sol deb na
Gang chän gon po tän zin gya tso yi
Ku tse mi shig kal gyar rab tän ching
Zhe dön lhun gyi drub par jin gyi lob

Chö ying kun säl khyon dang nyam jug pa'i
Dul dral de chen ye she gyu ma'i tin
Drang me ten dang ten pa'i kyil khor du
Shar wa'i yi dam lha tsog tham chä la

Dag chag dung shug drag pö sol deb na
Gang chän gon po tän zin gya tso yi
Ku tse mi shig kal gyar rab tän ching
Zhe dön lhun gyi drub par jin gyi lob

Pang tog yon tän lhun zog trin lä kyi
Nang wa dro kham gya tsor tag tsen pä
Phän dzä tob chu ngag wang lha yi lha
Rab jam dü sum gyal wa tham chäd la

Dag chag dung shug drag pö sol deb na
Gang chän gon po tän zin gya tso yi
Ku tse mi shig kal gyar rab tän ching
Zhe dön lhun gyi drub par jin gyi lob

Jig ten sum lä gang gi nge drol zhing
Chog tu shi wa nam jang nor bu'i ter
Zag me mi yo kun zang ge wa'i päl
Theg sum dam pa'i chö kyi tsog nam la

Dag chag dung shug drag pö sol deb na
Gang chän gon po tän zin gya tso yi
Ku tse mi shig kal gyar rab tän ching
Zhe dön lhun gyi drub par jin gyi lob

Srid pa'i trul khor jom la che pa wa'i
Den don ngon sum jal wa'i ye she chän
Nam thar dor je drong lä mi che pa
Rig drol phag pa'i ge dun tham che la

Dag chag dung shug drag pö sol deb na
Gang chän gon po tän zin gya tso yi
Ku tse mi shig kal gyar rab tän ching
Zhe dön lhun gyi drub par jin gyi lob

Kha chod zhing dang nä yul dur khro du
De tong nyam gyar rol pa'i tse jo yi
Näl jor lam zang drub la drog dzä pa'i
Nä sum pa wo kha dro'i tsog nam la

Dag chag dung shug drag pö sol deb na
Gang chän gon po tän zin gya tso yi
Ku tse mi shig kal gyar rab tän ching
Zhe dön lhun gyi drub par jin gyi lob

Dor je chang gi ka tag chag gya'i düd
Mi dral ral pa'i thöd du nyer köd nä
Tän dang tän dzin kyong wa'i thu tsal chän
Ye she chän dän tän srung gya tso la

Dag chag dung shug drag pö sol deb na
Gang chän gon po tän zin gya tso yi
Ku tse mi shig kal gyar rab tän ching
Zhe dön lhun gyi drub par jin gyi lob
De tar lu me kyab kyi chog nam la

Shug drag nying nä gu pä sol tab thü
Mi zä nyig ma'i zug du rab nar wa'i
Dag sog gang jong dro wa'i gon chig pu
Ngag wang lo zang tän zin gya tso chog
Sang sum mi shig mi gyur mi nub par
Zhom zhing yong dral dor je nying po'i tir
Kal pa gya tsor yo me tag tän shog

Rab jam gyal wa kun gyi dzä pa'i khur
Nying tob drag par zung wa'i lab chen gyi
Trin lä kun phän nor bu'i nying po chän
Zhe pa ji shin lhun gyi drub gyur chig

De thü zog dän kal zang nam kha'i go
Lü chän ngal so'i yi du tag drol shing
Thub tän chog dü kun tu rab dar wa'i
Ge tsän sid zhi'i tse mor gyä gyur chig

Chag na päd mo'i jin lab dud tsi'i gyun
Dag sog nying gi zug su tag min ching
Ka zhin drub pa'i chöd pä rab nyen nä
Kun zang chod chog gya tso thar son shog

Mä jung sä chä gyal wa'i jin lab dang
Ten drel lu wa me pa'i den pa dang
Dag gi lhag sam dag pa'i thü tob kyi
Mön pa'i dön kun de lag myur dub shog

Source: *www.tibet.com*

OM SVASTI (ENGLISH TRANSLATION)

To the assembly of most kind teachers, both present and past – the miraculous dance of the body, speech and mind of innumerable Buddhas manifesting in accord with aspirants' spiritual capacities, the wish-granting jewel, the source of all virtue and goodness – to you, we offer our prayers with fervent devotion:

That Tenzin Gyatso, protector of the Land of Snows, live for a hundred aeons. Shower on him your blessings so that his aspirations are fulfilled without hindrance.

To the assembly of all meditational deities manifesting as countless mandalas and divinities – the magical clouds of immaculate, transcendent wisdom reaching to the farthest expanse of the space of ultimate reality – to you, we offer our prayers with fervent devotion:

That Tenzin Gyatso, protector of the Land of Snows, live for a hundred aeons. Shower on him your blessings so that his aspirations are fulfilled without hindrance.

To all the victorious Buddhas of the three times endowed with ten powers and who are even masters of the gods, and whose attributes of perfection are the source of all compassionate deeds benefiting the vast ocean-like realm of sentient beings, to you, we offer our prayers with fervent devotion:

That Tenzin Gyatso, protector of the Land of Snows, live for a hundred aeons. Shower on him your blessings so that his aspirations are fulfilled without hindrance.

To the assembly of sacred doctrine embodied in the Three Vehicles, supremely serene, a jewel-treasure of enlightenment, stainless, unchanging, eternally good, and the glory of all virtues, which actually liberates beings from the sufferings of the three worlds, to you, we offer our prayers with fervent devotion:

That Tenzin Gyatso, protector of the Land of Snows, live for a hundred aeons. Shower on him your blessings so that his aspirations are fulfilled without hindrance.

To all members of the enlightening, noble spiritual community, who never stray from the thoroughly liberating adamantine city, who possess the wisdom eye that directly sees the profound truth and the highest valour to destroy all machinations of cyclic existence, to you, we offer our prayers with fervent devotion:

That Tenzin Gyatso, protector of the Land of Snows, live for a hundred aeons. Shower on him your blessings so that his aspirations are fulfilled without hindrance.

To the assembly of heroes and dakinis, heavenly beings of the three worlds, who appear in the highest paradises, in the sacred places, and in the cremation grounds, and who, through creative play in the hundred-fold experiences of bliss and emptiness, support practitioners in their meditation on the excellent path, to you, we offer our prayers with fervent devotion:

That Tenzin Gyatso, protector of the Land of Snows, live for a hundred aeons. Shower on him your blessings so that his aspirations are fulfilled without hindrance.

To the ocean of protectors endowed with eyes of transcendent wisdom – the powerful guardians and upholders of the teaching who wear inseparably on their matted locks the knot symbolising their pledge to the 'Vajra Holder' – to you, we offer our prayers with fervent devotion:

That Tenzin Gyatso, protector of the Land of Snows, live for a hundred aeons. Shower on him your blessings so that his aspirations are fulfilled without hindrance.

Thus to this congregation of excellent, undeceiving refuge, we pray that by the power of this prayer expressed from a heart filled with fervent devotion and humility, may the body, speech and mind of the sole of the Land of Snows, the supreme Ngawang Lobsang Tenzin Gyatso, be indestructible, unfluctuating and unceasing; may he live immutable for a hundred aeons, seated on a diamond throne, transcending decay and destruction.

You are the jewel-heart embodying all compassionate, beneficial deeds; O most courageous one, you carry upon your shoulders the burden of all the Buddhas of the infinite realms. May all your noble aspirations be fulfilled as intended.

By virtue of this may the heavenly doors of the fortunate era open eternally as a source of relief and respite for all beings; And may the auspicious signs reach the apex of existence and release, as the sacred teachings flourish through all times and in all realms.

May the nectar-stream of the blessings of the 'Lotus Holder' always enter our hearts and nourish it with strength. May we please you with our offerings of dedicated practice, And may we reach beyond the shores of perfect, compassionate deeds.

Through the blessings of the wondrous Buddhas and Bodhisattvas, by the infallible truth of the laws of dependent origination, and by the purity of our fervent aspirations, may the aims of my prayer be fulfilled without hindrance.

(Taken from *www.tibet.com*. English translation by Dr Thupten Jinpa Langri)

ENDNOTES

Part 1

1 Norbu, Jamyang. *Warriors of Tibet: The Story of Aten and the Khampa's Fight for the Freedom of Their Country*, pp. 104-105.
2 Interview with Kasur Juchen Thupten conducted on 21 January 2009 in his house in Dharamsala. In 1972, he came to Dharamsala and was Parliament member of Dotoe, speaker of Parliament till 1976. From 1976 till 1983, he was a Minister, then he became Prime Minister till 1991. He was the Chairman of the first delegation of the Tibetan government in exile that went to China, he returned in 1982 and in 1984. In 1992, he was the Chairman of the Tibetan Constitution Committee for five years. He wrote his autobiography which will be published soon.
3 Dunham, M. *Buddha's Warriors. The Story of the CIA-backed Tibetan Freedom Fighters, the Chinese Invasion, and the Ultimate Fall of Tibet*, pp. 166-167.
4 Craig, M. *Tears of Blood. A cry for Tibet*, p. 76.
5 Interview with Ringchen Tsering conducted on 6 February 2009 in his house in New Delhi. On 1 September 1960, he became member of Parliament of the Tibetan government in exile in Dharamsala.
6 Shakya, Tsering. *The Dragon in the Land of Snows,* pp. 144-147: In 1952 the anti-China movement, Mimang Tshongdu, saw the light in Lhasa after the inflation on grains, meat and household items. Soon the Chinese ordered them to disband and the Dalai Lama was forced to dismiss his two pro-independence prime Ministers.

   In 1954, on the eve of the Dalai Lama's visit to China, the group was recreated in order to persuade him not to go and because of the resentment against the erosion of his authority. The Mimang Tshongdu achieved popularity and received covert support from the Kashag since they thought it would enable the Tibetan government to put pressure on the Chinese. In spring 1956 the three leaders of the Mimang were arrested and detained for several months. One of them died in prison while the two others escaped to India after their release.
7 *Four Rivers, Six Ranges.* Autobiography of Andrug Gompo Tashi. One tola is equal to 11.66 grams.
8 Interview with Kasur Juchen Thupten.
9 The four rivers are the Dzachu or Mekong, the Drichu or Yangtze, the Nyalchu or Salween and the Machu or Huang Ho. The six mountains are the Duldza Zalmogang, Markhamgang, Pobargang, Mardzagang, Tshawagang and Minyagang. 'Four Rivers, Six Ranges' is an ancient name for Kham.
10 Brief Introduction of Chushi Gangdrug Defend Tibet Volunteer Force and Welfare Society of Central Dhokham Chushi Gangdrug of Tibet, pp. 3-4.
11 Peissel, M. *Cavaliers of Kham. The Secret War in Tibet,* p. 106.

12   Interview with Donyo Jagortsang conducted on 30 January 2009 in his office in Bir (Himachal Pradesh). He stayed in Darjeeling till 1964 taking some English tuition, then came to Dharamsala for about one year, then went to school in Mussoorie for about two to three years, went to Bir in 1966 where a Tibetan settlement was established. In 1968, he got the chance to go to the US for further studies, he returned in 1977 and is staying in Bir since that time.

13   Avedon, J. F. *In Exile from the Land of Snows. The Definitive Account of the Dalai Lama and Tibet Since the Chinese Conquest*, p. 120 gives a more detailed description about the training.

14   Interview with Donyo Jagortsang.

15   Interview with Donyo Jagortsang.

16   Interview with Kasur Juchen Thupten.

17   Interview with Donyo Jagortsang.

18   *Freedom in Exile. The Autobiography of the Dalai Lama of Tibet*, p. 140.

19   The Monlam ('prayer') festival is the greatest of the religious festivals in Tibet and lasts from the first till the 15th day of the first month of the lunar year.

20   Interview with Kasur Juchen Thupten.

21   Chakpori is a hill at 300 m south-west of the Potala Palace. During the seventeenth century, a temple was erected on the top of the mountain; inside was a statue of a Tibetan Medicine King who was believed to be an avatar of Sakyamuni and able to treat patients no matter what disease they had. Desi Sangye Gyatso, for twenty-six years the regent of the 5th Dalai Lama (1642-1682), founded the Tibetan Medical College in 1696. The building was demolished by the Chinese in 1959. The Tibetan government in exile rebuilt the Chakpori College in Darjeeling (India).

22   Interview with Kasur Juchen Thupten.

23   Excerpts from *My Land and My People*, pp. 200-216.

24   Interview conducted on 13 February 2009 in India, this person wanted to stay anonymous.

25   *My Land and My People. Memoirs of the Dalai Lama*, pp. 164-199: complete Uprising story.

26   *Freedom in Exile*, p. 162.

27   Knaus, J. K. *Orphans of the Cold War. America and the Tibetan Struggle for Survival*, p. 155.

28   Interview with Donyo Jagortsang.

29   Interview with Donyo Jagortsang.

30   Peissel, M. o.c., p. 156.

31   Avedon, J. F. o.c., p. 78.

32   Interview with Ringchen Tsering.

33   Interview with Ringchen Tsering.

34   Unless otherwise mentioned all the information in the chapters 'Strategy, Army life and Army rules' is translated from: Tsering, Tsongkha Lhamo. *Resistance, volume III: An Account of the Establishment of the Tibetan National Volunteer Defence Force in Mustang and Operations against the Communist Chinese inside Tibet: Part I* (in Tibetan language).

35   Interview with Ringchen Tsering.

36   Peissel, M. o.c., p. 219 & 227.

37   Exhaustive description of the 21 rules: Tsongkha Lhamo Tsering, o.c., pp. 136-141.

38   Knaus, J. K. o.c., p. 273.

39   Interview with Geshe Yungdrung Gyaltsen, president of Chushi Gangdruk in India, conducted on 16 January 2009 in their Delhi office. He will publish a book in Tibetan about the history of the organisation: *The truth about the History of the Dhokham Chushi Gangdruk Warriors against the Chinese.*

40   Basnyat, Dr Prem Singh. *Nepalese Army in Tibetan Khampa Disarming Mission*, pp. 4-5; pp.17-35: pictures of the captured weapons.

41   Sonam, Tenzing. *www.tibetwrites.org*: 'A Cold War in Shangri La'.

42   Ibidem.
43   Ibidem.
44   Knaus, J. K. o.c., pp. 316-317.
45   *Freedom in Exile*, pp. 210-12.
46   *Uncompromising Truth for a Compromised World: Tibetan Buddhism and Today's World*. Conceived, recorded and edited by Roebert Donavan, p. 97.
47   TibetInfonet Update 7 September 2005: USA plans to resettle Tibetan refugees from Nepal.
48   The Chushi Gangdruk has branches in Asia (India, Ladakh, Nepal, Bhutan, Taiwan & Japan), North America (US & Canada) and Europe (Belgium & Switzerland). For their websites: see the bibliography at the end.
49   *www.chushigangdruk.org*
50   Interview with Kasur Juchen Thupten.
51   *Phayul News* 1 July 2008: 'Fifty years of Chushi Gangdruk Commemorated in New York City', by Tenzin Choephel.
52   Interview with Kasur Juchen Thupten.
53   Interview with Donyo Jagortsang.
54   More information about the establishment of the settlements: *Tibet's Stateless Nationals: Tibetan Refugees in Nepal. Report of the Tibet Justice Center*, pp. 33-38.

Part 2

• WANGYAL
  1   These elections took place in October 2007. Mr Wangyal was re-elected as Lo-Drik-Tsug's president while Mr Tsering Siten (interview 46) became Settlement Officer of Jampaling, Paljorling and Tashigang.
• LOBSANG PHAKPA
  1   Throughout the interviews several place names are mentioned like Kesangbug, Yarabug, Tangebug; these place names were given by the Tibetans while staying there. Bug means 'inside'.
• TASHI
  1   In the Kongpo area there are sixty-five varieties of this tree; some flowers are used as medicine for blood circulation.
  2   More on this controversy on *http://www.dalailama.com*.
• AHNZIN
  1   J. Norbu, o.c., p. 11: In Tibet a man is often given a diminutive name of two syllables: the first syllable being the vowel AH of the Tibetan alphabet. In its religious context, AH is the root, the primordial sound.
  2   In Tibet several brothers can share a wife to safeguard the property and preserve the solidarity of the family.
• GOMPO
  1   In His negotiations with the Chinese leaders the Dalai Lama favours genuine autonomy for Tibet and no independence. This approach is called the 'Middle Way' (in Tibetan 'Umey lam').
• LHUNDUP TSONDU
  1   Tibetans wore several forms of protection of different sizes filled with precious relics; some contained a picture of the Dalai Lama or another Lama and small statues of Buddha, Manjushree and protection cords ('gawu'); others had no picture ('Tso Sung').
• KELSANG TSERING
  1   Shurdig is a place in Mustang; the name is given by the Tibetans, it's derived from 'shugpa', the Tibetan word for juniper.

● LOBSANG MONLAM

1　These books are the Tibetan Buddhist canon and contain the teachings of Buddha. The Library of Tibetan Works & Archives (LTWA) in Dharamsala has several handwritten editions of these books.

2　A ngul-dayen is a big silver coin of the Chinese with Mao's head on one side; at that time they used no paper money.

● TASHI TOPGYAL

1　There is some confusion here since Siling was not the name of the army leader, but Silingpu is the name of the army camp. The name of the Chinese General is Dan Guansan (Avedon, J. p. 49).

2　Since the names of the Nepalese Prime Ministers at that time were Kirti Nidhi Bista (1971-1973) and Nagendra Prasad Nijal (1973-1975), he probably refers to one of the commanders in charge.

● CHIME PHUNTSOK

1　The two pictures mentioned here can be seen on the cover page and opposite p.16. in the book of Dewatshang, Kunga Samten.

● SANGYE GONPO

1　This monastery is the Samdeling monastery on the outskirts of Kathmandu. A Mongolian abbot (kenpo) used to live there.

● JAMPA NORBU

1　Name for all protectors including Palden Lhamo and Nechung Choegyal, protector gods of the Dalai Lama.

2　In Peissel, M. p. 215 we can read a description of the village Kag: 'Kag was the first of the many typically Tibetan villages of the upper Kali Gandaki, built like a fort whose bastions are composed of the blank outer walls of the houses set one against the other. One enters the village by tunnels that burrow through the houses [...] It was the centre for the distribution and supply of wood to all the local army camps.'

● GYURME DORJEE

1　The most famous Tibetan mantra of Chenrezig, the Boddhisattva of Compassion, often translated as 'hail the jewel in the lotus'.

● DHONDUP TSERING

1　Bangladesh = East Pakistan. On 3 December 1971, Pakistan attacked India. The Indian Army overran the enemy and two weeks later the war was already over. Read more on *www.subcontinent.com/1971war*.

GLOSSARY

Amdo = one of the three traditional provinces of Tibet, comprises all those areas which are situated fully within the precincts of the Ma Chu River drainage area – as the upper reaches of the Yellow River are called in Tibetan. Most of those regions belong to the present-day Chinese province of Qinghai. Amdo was and is the home of many important Buddhist monks; the XIVth Dalai Lama, Tenzin Gyatso was born in Amdo. It is also called the province of horses since there are many different sorts of horses. The two other provinces are Kham and U-Tsang.

Amdowa(s) = inhabitants of the region Amdo.

Chushi Gangdruk = name of the Tibetan resistance organisation founded on 16 June 1958 by Andrug Gompo Tashi. Its name means 'Four Rivers, Six Ranges'. Most of its members were originated from Kham. The four rivers are the Dzachu (Mekong), the Drichu (Yangtze), the Nyalchu (Salween) and the Machu (Huang Ho); the six mountains are the Duldza Zalmogang, the Markhamgang, the Pobargang, the Mardzagang, the Tshawagang and the Minyagang.

Dhome = synonym for Amdo.

Dotoe = synonym for Kham.

dri = female yak.

Drepung = monastery at the outskirts of Lhasa, one of the three great Gelugpa (Yellow Hats) monasteries of Tibet next to Sera and Ganden. It is the largest of all monasteries and was founded in 1416. In former times it housed between 7,000 and 10,000 monks. It was called the Nalanda of Tibet, a reference to the great monastic university of India. In Mundgod, Karnataka (south India), the Tibetans re-established this monastery. (source: *Wikipedia Encyclopedia*)

drokpa = Tibetan word for nomad.

dzo/dzomo = cross-breeding between a yak/female yak and a domestic cow.

Ganden = one of the three great Gelugpa (Yellow Hats) monasteries of Tibet next to Sera and Drepung, located at 36 kms from Lhasa. It was the original monastery of the Gelugpa founded by its founder Je Tsongkapa himself. In the early twentieth century, 6,000 monks lived there, but only 2,000 in 1959. It has been re-established in Mundgod, Karnataka (south India). (source: *Wikipedia Encyclopedia*)

Gawu = a metal charm-box worn by the warriors to protect them. They contain relics blessed by a Lama and a picture of the Dalai Lama.

Gen = teacher; also used to speak in a respectful way of somebody.

Geshe = 'spiritual friend', though it is most often translated doctor of Buddhist philosophy or master of metaphysics. The Geshe degree requires intensive study and usually takes more than twenty years. It is emphasized primarily by the Gelugkpa tradition, but is also awarded in the Sakya and Bon schools. For a detailed description of the test: see AVEDON, J.F., pp. 49-50.

Gompa = Tibetan word for monastery. The design and interior details can vary from region to region, however, all follow a general sacred geometrical mandala design of a central praying hall and attached living accommodation. The gompa may also be accompanied by a number of stupas. A gompa can also be just a meditation hall. (source: *Wikipedia Encyclopedia*)

Gyalwa Rinpoche = His Holiness; name used by Tibetans when they speak about the Dalai Lama or the Karmapa.

Jabmak = Tibetan word for guerrilla fighter; in fact somebody who secretly attacks.

Kashag = the Tibetan Cabinet.

Kham = one of the three traditional provinces of Tibet, comprising the whole of south-eastern Tibet. It is also called 'the province of men', since the Khampas are known as brave warriors.

Khampa(s) = inhabitants of the region of Kham. They are known and feared as excellent warriors. They are tall, handsome, always carry a sword and are equestrians without equal. They often wear their hair elaborately braided and tied up with a red silk string.

Kunchoksum = the three Jewels: the Buddha, the Dharma (the teachings of Buddha) and the Sangha (the monastic community).

Lo-Drik-Tsug or Lodrik = a new resistance organisation that was established in 1960 in Mustang to fight against the Chinese in Tibet. It consisted of people of the three provinces Kham, Amdo and U-Tsang.

Lo = the Tibetan name for Mustang, an area in Nepal along the border with Tibet.

Mala = a Sanskrit word for a set of beads commonly used by Hindus and Buddhists, usually made from 108 beads. Malas are used for keeping count while reciting, chanting, or mentally repeating a mantra or the name or names of a deity. This practice is known in Sanskrit as 'japa' (source: *Wikipedia Encyclopedia*). The Tibetan word is 'trengwa'.

Mustang = Lo in Tibetan. It was once an independent kingdom, although closely tied by language and culture to Tibet. From the fifteenth century to the seventeenth century, its strategic location granted Mustang control over the trade between the Himalayas and India. By the end of the eighteenth century, the kingdom was annexed by Nepal. However, the monarchy still survives as the Kingdom of Lo in Upper-Mustang, with its capital at Lo Monthang. (source: *Wikipedia Encyclopedia*)

Norbulingka = summer palace of the Dalai Lama, originally built by the VIIIth Dalai Lama in the eighteenth century, located a few kilometres west of Lhasa. The Dalai Lamas ruled and received officials here from March till October. In 2001, the UNESCO (United Nations Educational, Scientific and Cultural Organisation) made it a World's Heritage Site as part of the 'Historic Ensemble of the Potala Palace'.

Potala = winter palace of the Dalai Lama, originally built by King Songtsen Gampo in the seventh century, it was rebuilt by the 5th Dalai Lama in 1645. It served as the seat of the Tibetan government and was the main residence of the Dalai Lama. The complex, which has a 1,000 rooms, has been turned into a museum; it remains a major pilgrimage site for Tibetan Buddhists.

Rupee(s) = Indian or Nepalese currency, 100 Rupees are worth respectively 1,50€ and 1€.

Sera = one of the three great Gelugpa (Yellow Hats) monasteries of Tibet next to Ganden and Drepung at 5 kms from Lhasa. In 1959, it housed more than 5,000 monks. After having been badly damaged during the Chinese invasion and the Cultural Revolution, it has been largely repaired and still housed 550 monks in 2008, but this number dropped to only a handful after the 2008 Uprising. (source: *Wikipedia Encyclopedia*)

Sherpas = trekking guides in the Himalaya region. They are often Sherpas, an ethnic group living in the mountains of eastern and central Nepal, originally from Tibet.

Tashi Delek = the common, everyday, Tibetan greeting, but it was not always so. Tashi means auspicious and delek means fine or well. It is properly used at the end of a message or meeting. The phrase means something like, "May everything be well" or "auspicious greetings." It is also used as a synonym for the word "greetings," so people are heard to say, "Many tashi deleks." (source: *www.khandro.net.*)

Thamzing = a 'struggle session', an inhuman and sadistic method that was used to denounce anybody of any authority: village headmen as well as lamas and landowners. The 'accused' victim was dragged onto a raised platform in a square in town and humiliated by the public. They were severely beaten before and during this session and often executed afterwards.

Tenshug = Long Life Ceremony; a long established Tibetan Buddhist ritual offered by followers to honour their teachers. It not only strengthens the bond between the spiritual teacher and disciple but also motivates the teacher to live longer. Those who participate in this offering ceremony do so with pure motivation and dedication. In order to free oneself from the cycle of births and deaths, one needs to have a guide who knows the way out, a guide whose knowledge is not merely gathered from books, but who himself has travelled the path to freedom. Otherwise, it will be a case of leading the blind. For a fortunate being who has met with such qualified teacher, it is indeed like finding a precious treasure. For the qualified teacher to remain with him as long as possible, one has to create the causes and conditions for that to happen. In Tibetan Buddhism, a traditional and formal way to create such causes and conditions is to hold a Long Life Ceremony for the teacher. (source: *www. saynyingon.org*) For a Tibetan and English version of the *Long Life Prayer for the Dalai Lama*, see appendix 2.

Tsampa = roasted barley flour.

Tso Sung = Tibetan silver or golden charm boxes in which were carried relics blessed by a Lama. It was believed that by carrying them, bullets would do no harm. *Tso* means sharp cutting instrument, sword or weapon, *Sung* means magic charm used as a protection against evil spirits as well as weapons.

Tung-wa = a cloth bundle worn around the neck, containing red protection cords and barley grains; resting on the chest or worn diagonal over one shoulder, blessed by the State Oracle; a talisman.

U-Tsang = one of the three traditional provinces of Tibet, Central Tibet, comprising the capital Lhasa; also called the province of religion due to the presence of the three great monasteries Sera, Drepung and Ganden.

A SELECTIVE BIBLIOGRAPHY

BOOKS IN ENGLISH

ANDRUGTSANG, Gompo Tashi. *Four Rivers, Six Ranges: Reminiscences of the Resistance Movement in Tibet*, Dharamsala, 1973.

AVEDON, John F. *In Exile from the Land of Snows. The Definitive Account of the Dalai Lama and Tibet Since the Chinese Conquest*, New York, 1997 (first edition 1984).

BASNYAT, Prem Singh Dr *Nepalese Army in Tibetan Khampa Disarming Mission*, Kathmandu, 2007.

CARTHY, R. Mc. *Tears of the Lotus. Accounts of Tibetan Resistance to the Chinese Invasion, 1950-1962*, USA, 1997.

CRAIG, Mary. *Tears of Blood. A Cry for Tibet*, New York, 1999.

DALAI LAMA, His Holiness. *Freedom in Exile: The Autobiography of the Dalai Lama of Tibet*, UK, 1990.

– *My Land and My People. Memoirs of the Dalai Lama of Tibet*, 4th Printing, New York and Dharamsala, 1992.

DEWATSHANG, Kunga Samten. *Flight At The Cuckoo's Behest. The Life and Times of a Tibetan Freedom Fighter as told to his son Dorjee Wangdi Dewatshang*, India, 1997.

DUNHAM, M. *Buddha's Warriors. The Story of the CIA-backed Tibetan Freedom Fighters, the Chinese Invasion, and the Ultimate Fall of Tibet*, USA, 2004. [With exhaustive bibliography]

FRENCH, Patrick. *Tibet, Tibet. A Personal History of a Lost Land*, New Delhi, 2003.

– *From the Roof of the World: Refugees of Tibet*, Berkeley California, 1992. [Comprises pictures of the arrival and early years of the Tibean refugees in India]

KNAUS, J. K. *Orphans of the Cold War: America and the Tibetan Struggle for Survival*, New York, 1999.

LAIRD, T. *The Story of Tibet. Conversations with the Dalai Lama*, London, 2006.

NORBU, Jamyang. *Warriors of Tibet: The Story of Aten and the Khampa's Fight for the Freedom of Their Country*, London, 1986.

NORBU, Tseten. *La Reconquête du Tibet*, Spain, 1999.

PEISSEL, M. *Cavaliers of Kham. The Secret War in Tibet*, London, 1972.

SHAKYA, Tsering.*The Dragon in the Land of Snows: a History of Modern Tibet since 1947*, London, 1999.

Tibet's Stateless Nationals Tibetan Refugees in Nepal. Tibet Justice Centre, June 2002.

Uncompromising Truth for a Compromised World: Tibetan Buddhism and Today's World. Conceived, recorded and edited by Donavan Roebert, USA, 2006.

BOOKS IN TIBETAN

TSERING, Tsonghka Lhamo. *Resistance, volume III: An Account of the Establishment of the Tibetan National Volunteer Defense Force in Mustang and Operations against the Communist Chinese inside Tibet: Part I and II*, Dharamsala, 2002.

Lithang Athar Norbu's Life Story, Delhi, 2004 (Autobiography, published after his death by his wife Phuntsok Choedon).

The Autobiography of Dasur Ratuk Ngawang of Lithang, Vol. 3 Part I and II, Dharamsala, 2008 (compiled and edited by Tashi Tsering).

Offerings to the Land of Snow. Bari Dawa Tsering, translated by Bawa Kelsang Gyaltsen and published by the Department of Information and International Relations, Dharamsala, 2008.

MAGAZINES

Brief Introduction of Chushi Gangdrug Defend Tibet Volunteer Force and Welfare Society of Central Dhokham Chushi Gangdrug of Tibet. 15 November 1998.

Incomparable Warriors. Non-violent Resistance in Contemporary Tibet. ICT, 2005.

NORBU, Jamyang. 'The Tibetan Resistance Movement and the Role of the C.I.A.. Part III Exile: Resistance and Diplomacy', in *Resistance and Reform in Tibet*. Ed. by Robert Barnett and Shirin Akiner, Delhi, 1994, pp. 186-196.

'The Escape that rocked the Reds', in *Time Magazine*, 20 April 1959 (cover story). The article can be read on *www.time.com/time/archive*.

MOVIES

CIA in Tibet. The inside story of Tibet's Guerrilla War against China and the covert CIA operation that backed it (currently in production). It is an inside look at the CIA's involvement with Tibet in their covert war with China from 1957 to 1973. This three-part documentary project is being produced by Lisa Cathey, the daughter of a former CIA case officer who worked on the Tibetan Task Force in India and Nepal. Combined with rare archival and personal footage, her father's never-before-told stories mix with other key players' accounts and diverse perspectives in this timely examination of a seminal time in Tibet's continuing struggle for independence from China. *www.ciaintibet.com*

The Shadow Circus. The CIA in Tibet. A film by Ritu Sarin and Tenzing Sonam. White Crane Film Production for BBC TV, 1998. *www. asianamericanmedia.org/shadowcircus*

Kundun. A film written by Melissa Mathison and directed by Martin Scorsese, Touchstone Pictures, USA, 1997. Film based on the life of the Dalai Lama (shows images of the Chinese invasion, the uprising in Lhasa and the flight of the Dalai Lama).

WEBSITES

www.tibetmap.com or *www.tibetmap.org*: site with several maps of Tibet.

www.chushigangdruk.org and *www.chushigangdruk.ca*: sites of the Chushi Gangdruk organisations.

www.dalailama.com: photo gallery/escape into exile: pictures of the Dalai Lama on his flight.

www.mikeldunham.blogs.com: blog of Mikel Dunham, author of *Buddha's Warriors*.

www.tibetwrites.org: 'a not-for-profit site dedicated to Tibet and Tibetan people':

– SONAM, Tenzing. *A Cold War in Shangri La – The CIA in Tibet*. Wednesday, 26 December 2007. (First published in Man's World, India, September 2000). NORBU, Jamyang. *The Forgotten Anniversary. Remembering the Great Khampa Uprising of 1956*. Thursday, 27 December 2007. (First published in December 2006)